THE TEN COMMANDMENTS AND HUMAN RIGHTS

OVERTURES TO BIBLICAL THEOLOGY
A series of studies in biblical theology designed
to explore fresh dimensions of research and to
suggest ways in which the biblical heritage may
address contemporary culture

Editors

WALTER BRUEGGEMANN, Dean of Academic
Affairs and Professor of Old Testament at
Eden Theological Seminary

JOHN R. DONAHUE, S.J., Associate Professor of
New Testament at Vanderbilt Divinity School

THE TEN COMMANDMENTS AND HUMAN RIGHTS

WALTER HARRELSON

FORTRESS PRESS   Philadelphia

Library of Congress Cataloging in Publication Data

Harrelson, Walter J
   The Ten commandments and human rights.

   (Overtures to Biblical theology)
   Includes indexes.
   1. Commandments, Ten. 2. Civil rights—Biblical teaching. 3. Church and civil rights—Biblical teaching. I. Title. II. Series.
BS1285.2.H37   241.5′2   77-15234
ISBN 0-8006-1527-1

6520E80   Printed in the United States of America   1–1527

To Marianne

Contents

Series Foreword

Biblical theology has been a significant part of modern study of the Jewish and Christian Scriptures. Prior to the ascendancy of historical criticism of the Bible in the nineteenth century, biblical theology was subordinated to the dogmatic concerns of the churches, and the Bible too often provided a storehouse of rigid proof texts. When biblical theology was cut loose from its moorings to dogmatic theology to become an enterprise seeking its own methods and categories, attention was directed to what the Bible itself had to say. A dogmatic concern was replaced by an historical one so that biblical theology was understood as an investigation of what was believed by different communities in different situations. By the end of the nineteenth century biblical theology was virtually equated with the history of the religion of the authors who produced biblical documents or of the communities which used them.

While these earlier perspectives have become more refined and sophisticated, they still describe the parameters of what is done in the name of biblical theology—moving somewhere between the normative statements of dogmatic theology and the descriptive concerns of the history of religions. Th. Vriezen, in his *An Outline of Old Testament Theology* (Dutch, 1949; ET, 1958), sought to combine these concerns by devoting the first half of his book to historical considerations and the second half to theological themes. But even that effort did not break out of the stalemate of categories. In more recent times Old Testament theology has been dominated by two paradigmatic works. In his *Theology of the Old Testament* (German, 1933–39; ET, 1967) W. Eichrodt has provided a comprehensive statement around fixed categories which reflect classical dogmatic interests, although the centrality of covenant in his work reflects the Bible's own categories. By contrast, G. von Rad in his *Old Testament Theology* (German, 1960; ET, 1965) has presented a study of theological traditions with a primary concern for the historical dynamism of the traditions. In the case of New Testament theology, historical and theological concerns are rather roughly juxtaposed in the work of A. Richardson, *An Introduction to the Theology of the New Testament*. As in the case of the Old Testament there are two major options or presentations which dominate in New Testament studies. The history-of-religion school has left its mark on the magisterial work of R. Bultmann, who proceeds from an explanation of the expressions of faith of the earliest communities and their theologians to a statement of how their understanding of existence under faith speaks to us today. The works of O. Cullmann and W. G. Kümmel are clear New Testament statements of *Heilsgeschichte* under the aegis of the tension between promise and fulfillment— categories reminiscent of von Rad.

As recently as 1962 K. Stendahl again underscored the tension between historical description and normative meaning by assigning to the biblical theologian the task of describing what the Bible *meant,* not what it *means* or *how* it can have meaning. However, this objectivity of historical description is too often found to be a mirror of the observer's hidden preunderstanding, and the adequacy of historical description is contingent on one generation's discoveries and postulates. Also, the yearning and expectation of believers and would-be believers will not let biblical theology rest with the descriptive task alone. The growing strength of Evangelical Protestantism and the expanding phenomenon of charismatic Catholicism are but vocal reminders that people seek in the Bible a source of alternative value systems. By its own character and by the place it occupies in our culture the Bible will not rest easy as merely an historical artifact.

Thus it seems a fitting time to make "overtures" concerning biblical theology. It is not a time for massive tomes which claim too much. It appears not even to be a time for firm conclusions which are too comprehensive. It is a time for pursuit of fresh hints, for exploration of new intuitions which may reach beyond old conclusions, set categories, and conventional methods. The books in this series are concerned not only with what is seen and heard, with what the Bible said, but also with what the Bible says and the ways in which seeing and hearing are done.

In putting forth these *Overtures* much remains unsettled. The certainties of the older biblical theology *in service* of dogmatics, as well as of the more recent biblical theology movement *in lieu* of dogmatics, are no longer present. Nor is there on the scene anyone of the stature of a von Rad or a Bultmann to offer a synthesis which commands the theological engagement of a generation and summons the church to a new restatement of the biblical message. In a period characterized by an information explosion the relation of analytic study to attempts at synthesis is unsettled. Also unsettled is the question whether the scholarly canon of the university or the passion of the confessing community provides a language and idiom of discourse, and equally unsettled—and unsettling—is the question whether biblical theology is simply one more specialization in an already fragmented study of Scripture or whether it is finally the point of it all.

But much remains clear. Not simply must the community of biblical scholars address fresh issues and articulate new categories for the well-being of our common professional task; equally urgent is the fact that the dominant intellectual tradition of the West seems now to carry less conviction and to satisfy only weakly the new measures of knowing which are among us. We do not know exactly what role the Bible will play in new theological statements or religious postures, nor what questions the Bible can and will address, but *Overtures* will provide a locus where soundings may be taken.

We not only intend that *Overtures* should make contact with people professionally involved in biblical studies, but hope that the series will speak to all who care about the heritage of the biblical tradition. We hope that the volumes will represent the best in a literary and historical study of biblical traditions without canonizing historical archaism. We hope also that the studies will be relevant without losing the mystery of biblical religion's historical distance, and that the studies touch on significant themes, motifs, and symbols of the Bible without losing the rich diversity of the biblical tradition. It is a time for normative literature which is not heavy-handed, but which seriously challenges not only our conclusions but also the shape of our questions.

Walter Harrelson, distinguished professor at the Divinity School of Vanderbilt University, here offers a fresh *Overture* to the study of the Ten Commandments. He does so by combining careful, critical exegetical work with attentive discernment of the needs and options in the present social context. Of course there is a rich supply of books on the Ten Commandments, but Harrelson probes beneath conventional exposition to reconsider the meaning of authority and the role of command in a religion of graciousness and a culture of self-preoccupation. Four characteristics of Harrelson's discussion indicate its freshness:

1. The book is at once profoundly conservative and yet shrewdly contemporary. It is conservative in that Harrelson does not seek to work around or explain away the claims of the commandments. He insists that they must be taken in their main and unchanging meaning. But Harrelson is contemporary in that he understands the temptations of modernity and the perceptual field in which ethics must now be done. He is clear that contemporary cultural reality has in no way diminished the pertinence or urgency of the biblical commandments. His sensitivity to current issues is evidenced by his inclusion of and appeal to the Universal Declaration of Human Rights. Indeed, linkage of the Ten Commandments to the issue of human rights (as reflected in the title) makes the discussion both conservative and contemporary.

2. Harrelson sees the Torah, and specifically the Decalogue, as the meeting place of Judaism and Christianity. That which divides and unites this family of faith is located in issues of law and obedience. The author has long been attentive to this issue.

He is bold enough to suggest that both Judaism and Christianity have a calling to protest against distortions of the other: "Judaism witnesses against a faithless Christianity or a triumphalist Christianity that claims more than its actual life supports. And Christianity may be able, when faithful, to witness against a Judaism that should be able to discern the consummation that God indeed has brought near" (pp. 171–72). While a complete harmony between Judaism and Christianity is remote, clearly the route to it is by way of these commandments.

3. Harrelson's exposition understands and takes into account the force of the Decalogue for the present and the envisioning of an alternative humanity which is implicit in the claims of the commandments. The Ten Commandments move back and forth between "already" and "not yet." Harrelson is realistic enough to know that it is the present human community for which ethical responsibility must be taken. But he is also believing and hopeful enough to affirm that the promised humanity of God will be characterized by the holiness and justice evoked by the commandments. Thus the commandments are the route of present people into the promised community. Harrelson will not let us choose between his realism and his hope.

4. This discussion is a full-fledged articulation of human freedom, a charter for free persons. And yet, faithful to Israel, Harrelson understands that full personal freedom can exist only in the context of a visible, bonded community. And so he characterizes the promised freedom of the commandments in the gospel song as freedom in captivity (p. 185):

> Make me a captive, Lord,
> And then I shall be free;
> Force me to render up my sword,
> And I shall conqueror be.

This discernment of freedom locates the author in the hard-nosed realism of Israel's vision but also in the passion of Christian piety. The two together are affirmed against a self-seeking and self-serving ethos that eschews obedience and unwittingly forfeits every real freedom.

These four points are enough to evidence that Harrelson is a

practical but uncompromised interpreter, a matured and knowing expositor, who does not flinch from Torah in a time which
would prefer either personalistic freedom or person-denying
authoritarianism (or both). The delicacy of nuance and the
passion for our faith situation make this an *Overture* bursting
with grace-filled surprises.

WALTER BRUEGGEMANN
JOHN R. DONAHUE, S.J.

Preface

The Bible knows little or nothing about human rights in our sense of the term. It does know and say a great deal about the obligations of individuals and of the human community to the Lord and Giver of life and to fellow human beings. But one's obligations to others are in fact the realities that the others have a right to expect. I am under obligation to be faithful to my wife, faithful in all the ways that the term has meaning. This means that my wife has a right to expect such faithfulness. God also has a right to expect such faithfulness!

In that sense, the Bible has much to say about human rights. It is possible to see in the basic understandings of human rights, reflected in, for example, the United Nations' Universal Declaration of Human Rights, a large measure of the biblical understanding of human obligation under God.

The legal materials of the Old Testament, and the Decalogue in particular, contain the foundation of much of this understanding of human rights, in the biblical sense of the term. In the present study the effort is made to show just how significant the Ten Commandments are for a biblical understanding of the rights of human beings in relation to others, and how significant they are for the New Testament and for contemporary human life today.

I would like to express my special thanks to several persons who have assisted me in the work here presented. The late Professor Isaac Mendelson of Columbia University and Professor Samuel Terrien of Union Theological Seminary in New York first aroused my interest in biblical and ancient Near Eastern law and taught me much. Professor Terrien kindly accepted my articles on Old Testament law which were edited by him and published in the *Interpreter's Dictionary of the Bible* in 1962.[1] Students at the University of Chicago Divinity School and at the Divinity School of Vanderbilt University have worked with me on the subject off and on for many years. Scholars at the Ecumenical Institute for Advanced Theological Studies in Jerusalem also participated with me in discussions of the subject and offered criticism of portions of the manuscript. A special word of thanks is owed to Professor Walter Brueggemann, editor of the series, for his many comments and suggestions. In addition, I would like to thank the members of the discussion group on the Bible and ethics at Vanderbilt University for their careful and discerning comments and criticisms of portions of the study. I would also like to thank the Reverend Michael Hurley, S.J., and the Irish School of Ecumenics, Dublin, for inviting me to participate in the November-December 1978 International Conference on Human Rights held in Dublin, and the Research Council of Vanderbilt University and the United Presbyterian Church in the U.S.A. for financial assistance in connection with that Conference.

A series of sermons on the Decalogue by Professor Gerhard Ebeling[2] helped me enormously in clarifying the value of the Decalogue for contemporary life, as well as the limits to applying the Decalogue to our own times and problems. A short book on the Decalogue by Dr. Helen Schüngel-Straumann, entitled *Der Dekalog—Gebot Gottes?*[3] came to my attention after I had completed the manuscript, but I found it immensely helpful and was able to make some changes in light of her excellent work.

My hope is that this study will encourage groups and individuals to look again at the biblical heritage for concrete guidance in their efforts to live responsibly and faithfully during times of great difficulty and challenge to the human community. I especially hope that this small work will contribute to a deepened understanding, on the part of Christians, of the Jewish religious heritage, which is so intimately interwoven with the Christian heritage. The truth of this interweaving was impressed upon me all the more deeply as I spent the last two years as a staff member of the Ecumenical Institute in Jerusalem, where the manuscript was finally completed. Christians if they do not know intimately the inner power and depth of God's demands—demands like those summarized in the Decalogue[4]—will never know the inner power and depth of the love of God for sinners while they are sinners. A right understanding of Torah, of Law in the sense of obligation under God, is essential for an understanding of the love and grace of God. May this study contribute to the furthering of that understanding.

Abbreviations

ANET	*Ancient Near Eastern Texts Relating to the Old Testament,* ed. James B. Pritchard, 2d ed. (Princeton: Princeton University Press, 1955)
ATANT	Abhandlungen zur Theologie des Alten und Neuen Testaments
BA	*Biblical Archaeologist*
BWANT	Beiträge zur Wissenschaft vom Alten und Neuen Testament
BZAW	Beihefte zur Zeitschrift für die alttestamentliche Wissenschaft
FRLANT	Forschungen zur Religion und Literatur des Alten und Neuen Testaments
IDB	*Interpreter's Dictionary of the Bible*
JBL	*Journal of Biblical Literature*
SBT	Studies in Biblical Theology
TB	Theologische Bücherei
VT	*Vetus Testamentum*
WMANT	Wissenschaftliche Monographien zum Alten und Neuen Testament
ZAW	*Zeitschrift für die alttestamentliche Wissenschaft*

PART ONE

HISTORICAL
AND STRUCTURAL
PROBLEMS

CHAPTER 1

The Ten
Commandments Today

Young men and women learned the Ten Commandments by heart as a part of catechism study in many Christian communities during the past centuries. The practice has not been abandoned, but it is probably quite rare these days in Western Christian lands for persons actually to know the contents of the Ten Commandments. There are gains in this loss, but there also are great losses.

We all know that Christianity has suffered greatly from a moralistic application of the Ten Commandments and other legal materials to personal and social life. So it is one of the great gains of the past three or four decades of Christian life in the West that much of this moralism and legalism has been exposed and largely overcome. The Ten Commandments contributed to the moralism and the legalism, and thus the loss of knowledge of them could be termed a gain.

At the same time, many persons in the Western world must surely believe that the loss of the Ten Commandments from our common life threatens to sweep away something vital. This is not because the Decalogue helped to maintain the old ways and customs of our forebears, not because we long to return to an earlier epoch when people really believed the Bible and followed its tenets. No, the loss of knowledge of the Ten Commandments means a loss in understanding what human liberty is, what freedom of the spirit means, and how freedom is to be maintained in the world.

My contention in this book is that our societies have indeed suffered a great and almost numbing loss now that these prohibitions no longer have a vital place, but it is not an irrecoverable loss. We cannot simply reassert that the Ten Commandments must be taken seriously and expect that it will come to pass, but we dare not be alarmist when advocating that the study of the Ten Commandments be again introduced into the curriculums of religious schools. Rather, we need quite soberly to seek to understand what these prohibitions, and others like them, have meant for earlier generations, including the generations of the biblical peoples. When we see what they once meant, and how important that meaning was, we can take steps to reclaim for our own generation this priceless part of the biblical heritage.

We shall have to reclaim this heritage in responsible ways. That means that we must proceed critically, examining this part of the biblical literature and heritage by seeking to understand what it once meant and struggling to weigh that meaning and determine whether it can and does have any meaning for us in our own social and personal existence today.

THE "OLD TESTAMENT" AS A BOOK OF LAW

First it is necessary to remove some of the difficulties that prevent us from hearing this message from the Hebrew Scriptures. Christians refer to the Hebrew Scriptures as the "Old Testament," but this entirely well-meant designation has done much harm. Once, as the early Christians were affirming the difference that the Christian revelation made, they contrasted the new reality with the "old things" that had passed away (see, e.g., 2 Cor. 5:14–21). The age of blessedness promised to the offspring of Israel had dawned; God had brought redemption to his people and to the world. No longer did people need to wait and hope, for that for which they waited and hoped had come to the world. It had come in the one whom God had raised from death, this Jesus of Nazareth who had been put to death by the Roman authorities with the support of some leaders of the Jewish community in Jerusalem.

But nowhere in the New Testament do we have direct warrant for calling the Scriptures of the Jewish people the "Old Testament" or the "Old Covenant," in contrast to the New. If the term is to be retained at all, it must be retained as a term for one part of the *Christian* Bible, and we must always be quick to point out that Christians use the term to refer to the *Jewish* Scriptures.

Along with the use of the term *Old* we have inherited another venerable but mischief-working distinction: the Old Testament has been identified as a book of the "law," in contrast to the New Testament, the Christian book of grace and free forgiveness. All informed Christians know that the Hebrew Scriptures are full of affirmations of the grace of God for sinners and that there is a vast body of literature in the Hebrew Scriptures that has nothing whatever to do with law in any meaning of the term. Yet the distinction continues to be drawn. Connected with it is the picture of the God of the Hebrew Scriptures as a God of stern demands for justice and wrath against all who fail to do right, in contrast to the picture of the God of the New Testament as a God of love and forgiveness.

As a result of this popular misrepresentation of the religion of the ancient Israelites, Christians have slowly lost appreciation for the value such materials as the Ten Commandments have in holding a society together. It is supposed that with the coming of the Christ the commandments have been reduced to two, and both of them positive: love God and love your neighbor. What need have we further for these older, largely negative commandments? Law can be such a coercive reality in social life; those in authority can simply sanctify the prohibitions they wish to see observed and keep in thralldom those who are bound to maintain allegiance to such prohibitions or positive commandments. Jesus' great breakthrough, it has been maintained, is precisely the liberating of the human spirit from such a negative religious outlook and from a religion of fear and law.

There is truth in such observations. Every religion can be turned into an unwholesome legalism and at some stages in its actual history is likely to have experienced such a fate. There have been the periods of Christian legalism that were perversions of the gospel of Christian liberty. It is also right to say that the Hebrew Scriptures do have much to do with law, with Torah, and that one of the valid distinctions between Judaism and Christianity is that Judaism understands itself as a religious movement tied to the absolute demands of God's Torah, God's authoritative teaching or guidance. Christianity, on the other hand, can rightly be seen as a religion in which an essential ingredient is the freedom of the human spirit with which God's raising of Jesus from death is inseparably connected. The Christian community of those who are witnesses of the Resurrection is a community marked by a new perception of the possibilities of human life and human community. Human beings need no longer live under compulsions and constraints that long have bound and sometimes enslaved them. They need no longer live only in hope of a time of freedom and joy and blessedness in God's presence. They need not do so, because what God has promised God now has brought to reality. Human beings need only to claim the glory and the new prospects for human life, individually and corporately, as they await the consummation of the day of fulfillment that is very near at hand. Is there any place for the Ten Commandments in such a community of the Resurrection? We intend to confront that question head-on, for it is one of the most weighty ones we will face.

THE "IRRELEVANCY" OF THE COMMANDMENTS
TO CONTEMPORARY LIFE

An even more serious obstacle to our coming to understand and appreciate the Ten Commandments in fresh ways today is the widespread belief that these commandments are of no further real use to contemporary men and women. In fact, this is a conclusion that is simply taken for granted. For example, in our secular world what possible meaning could a commandment that prohibits the worship of other gods have? Our generation seems to have managed its affairs successfully without belief in any god at all. To hold up for persons the first commandment, with its call to hold fast to the worship of Yahweh (the personal name for the God of Israel) and to let Yahweh have no rivals at all in in our lives—what could that possibly mean concretely? Or to prohibit making images of God, something our generation has certainly not the slightest temptation to do, would seem a clear absurdity. The sanctifying of the Sabbath Day may be all right for the state of Israel, but in most Western lands we have already established the five-day work week, which gives at least two free days for leisure and for such engagements as men and women may see fit to pursue. It would be quaint to hold up Sabbath observance in the modern, industrialized world, where the large question is how to adjust the realities of the society to a continuingly diminishing need for human physical labors. A real question is what to do with our leisure, not how to get people to stop working on some sacral day.

The prohibition against acts of adultery would seem to many not only pointless—since sexual practices have undergone revolutionary changes in the past few decades and are certainly not likely to be modified by some call to avoid adultery—but in fact wrong. Have we not finally begun to identify human sexuality as as a natural good of life and to free it from the prejudiced weight of a negative religiosity? A commandment against adultery surely may be all right as a reminder of the importance of family life today, but as the central commandment of a sexual ethic would it not be ludicrous to argue for its reinstatement?

Regarding the protection of property that seems to be central to the commandments about stealing and coveting, sensitive Christians today may feel that we do not need any further religious demands in that direction, but rather a deeper commitment to sharing the goods of the earth more widely and more fairly. A capitalist society might well use such commandments to seek to protect its holdings, but what has such an effort to do with Christian faith?

As Gerhard Ebeling has pointed out in a marvelous series of sermons on the Ten Commandments,[1] we may be left with one commandment that has validity: the commandment against killing. That commandment surely will never lose its value or its relevancy to contemporary life. But the vast majority of the commandments in the Decalogue, it would appear, either have no real bearing on our present life or seem capable of damaging that life if they were reintroduced.

NEGATIVE, LEGALISTIC RELIGION

We all can have some sympathy for the belief that the moralism and legalism of the church in the past have been the cause of much harm. There is no doubt at all that religious communities throughout the centuries have in many cases served to keep certain groups within a society in subjection to other groups. Religion has been used as a sanction for unjust norms, as an instrument for enslavement rather than freedom. And a religion that is on the whole open and positive about life can easily fall victim to petty legalisms. One need only examine various efforts in Christian history to establish an authoritarian religious society on earth to see the damage that can be done to human beings. When the society is regulated in detail by positive legal requirements or by negatively framed prohibitions, the society often has thereby made a travesty of the human freedom that is intended to issue from God's gift of Torah. Nothing in the pages that follow is intended to serve the cause of a narrow legalism or authoritarian religious pretensions.

The problem lies, as we shall see, not in the negative form of such commandments and not in their availability as summary statements of what the God of the covenant requires of the people of God, but in the way in which the community comes to understand such summaries and such negative formulas. Calvin's Geneva was not in the least made unwholesome by the requirement that all citizens hold fast the tenets of the Decalogue.[2] John Winthrop's New England was not ruined by the negatively framed summaries of the divine law. The damage lay, rather, in a spirit of fear and repression, in a commitment to make all human beings conform to the positive demands believed to issue from the divine law.

THE NEED FOR CREDIBLE AND
DURABLE NORMS

If we look deeply into our own lives and test carefully the anxieties and concerns of our fellow citizens, we may be willing to explore what value the absolute norms and prohibitions that appear in the Ten Commandments may have. Men and women today do have a profound longing for a set of norms that can be relied upon. What kinds of conduct are simply not possible to the Christian man or woman? What is "the good life" for the

Christian family today? How can we teach our children anything that we can claim to be absolutely right and binding for all of life? Is there really any such thing as a set of basic, concrete guidelines for the Christian community today?

In contemporary, secularized Western society there is a wistful longing for such norms, upon which individual and family could depend in all circumstances. One reason for the rapid growth today of evangelical religion of a fundamentalist nature, or for the growth of charismatic religion, with its rigid personal and communal norms, is that such communities are thought to supply just such norms. Not all the norms supplied in these communities are perceived to be rigid or authoritarian. In fact, in some of the evangelical and orthodox Christian movements there appears to be a deep appreciation of the positive import of such prohibitions and a determination to avoid rigidity and authoritarianism as the community recommits itself to fixed, "biblical" norms.

We should know, however, that if we are to find a way to supply nourishment to meet this hunger, we have to do so with the utmost care. The gains of a contextualist and existentialist ethic are too numerous and too solid to be endangered by facile returns to absolutist norms. The enslavement of the human spirit in the name of religion is too well known in history. We dare not risk a recurrence of such enslavement out of fear that our society is about to collapse into normlessness. And the misuse of norms for the protection of the privileged is a perennial danger.

Nonetheless, the situation of human beings in the Western world, and of families and of societies as well, is so desperately grave that some risks have to be taken. We have clearly gone too far into sentimental lawlessness in the name of love and mercy. We have let slip away from us the biblical picture of a God who cares fiercely about justice on earth and will not forever permit injustice to continue.[3] The religious community has to maintain both its social ethic and its personal ethic, its fidelity to the tenets of prophetic religion with its social norms, and its fidelity to the demands of God upon the individual. Some way has to be found to describe in credible ways the absolutely binding claim of the God of biblical faith upon the religious community and the individual. The freedom that is God's gift of love to people and community is a freedom that is reciprocally related to the absolute claim of God upon community and individual.

It is worth our while, therefore, to attempt to test the value of this ancient set of short, pithy prohibitions found in the Ten Commandments. We need norms that are credible and durable. Perhaps we will find that these ancient norms that have been of great value to past generations do in fact continue to have great value.

DISTINCTIVE FEATURES OF THESE NORMS

Norms of the sort we long for are usually provided within a human community quite naturally. Children grow up in a society in which they absorb a way of life, a way of conduct, and a way of relating to fellow members of the community, to the practices of the community, and to the natural order. Just as children are "taught" what they like by way of food, what occupations they prefer, and what relations they appreciate most between members of their own sex and members of the opposite sex, so also they are "taught" the norms that pertain to adultery, killing, stealing, bearing false witness, and the like. There is nothing at all mysterious about the process of acculturization, by means of which persons enter into adulthood, over time, within a fixed community's own norms, many if not all of which may in some societies not even be written down.

This process of providing clues to our children goes on in modern Western societies as well. We teach our children manners and morals, on one very important level, without setting out to do so at all. Most of the shaping of members of the community for the normative life they are to live is done without any direct effort to teach norms or to lay down the demands of God upon them. Indeed, no society has time to teach everything explicitly, and norms are too important to be left to the schools. They must be taken in along with the mother's milk; they must be as unmistakable a part of the life of a young boy or girl as the reliability of the parents in time of need.

There do develop situations, however, in which a society must be more explicit about certain norms. These situations often occur when there is a confrontation with a rival community or society, or a move from one location to another, with social and cultural changes taking place. Or, as in the modern world, the emergence of fluidity or rapid social change in the society will require a more explicit set of norms.

As many social analysts have pointed out, contemporary Western society is so fluid, so much on the move, and subject to such rapid social change that there seems to be no way for the society to "freeze" the situation long enough for the members of the community to pass along their lore to a new generation. The conflict among the rival communities and cultures is so severe that even if there were time the present generation would have great difficulty claiming the attention of the new generation long enough to pass on the norms.

Moreover, there has certainly developed in course of this rapid social change an attitude toward change that is different from any that ever was known in the world. Change is greeted with much less ambivalence in the contemporary Western world than is common within societies. We might say that young men and women today assume that almost all change is likely to be for the good of the society. If a norm or custom has been in effect for a long time, and if it is prized by the older generation, that is enough to make it suspect.

Such an attitude has its wholesome side, but it is devastating, given the situation within which most Western families must compete for the attention of the young in providing the norms for life in which they believe and which they are convinced their children should observe. So little time is available, and when the parents, even though loved and respected, are not seen as real authorities for life in our world for the coming decades, how can the children take the norms from them in the way that earlier generations were able to do? Our children know from firsthand experience that their parents, most of them, still hold to an outmoded approach to mathematics. They have outmoded tastes in music. They have only a limited grasp of the contemporary technological civilization within which they live and on which they depend. What do our parents know that is really reliable and that we should accept from them with little or no questioning? Perhaps only such things as whether or not we have the money, as a family, to afford some of the things we would like to have. Otherwise, our parents' world is not our world, and their norms are not our norms.

Small wonder that in such a situation it would only worsen the guilt of most parents if we should urge upon them the necessity of imposing upon their children the ancient norms of the Ten Commandments, or some comparable set of norms. If our view that such norms are essential to the health of the society is to be accepted, it must be accepted with some hints, at least, as to how such norms might be laid hold of by the contemporary generations. And it must be indicated how the self-imposition and mutual imposition of such norms (they cannot be imposed entirely from "outside") can in fact help meet the deep and urgent need so many of us feel for these credible and durable norms.

The norms we have in our Ten Commandments and in comparable lists are often short and frequently negative. They are easily remembered and may well be associated with some mnemonic device or other. They have to be quite general but must at the same time be concrete and refer to known and clear features of the common life. They must deal with elements of the society that most people can recognize to be significant, not banal. And they must allow for interpretation. If there is anything absolutely self-evident in them, they quickly come to be viewed as banal. There must be the possibility of disagreement as to what they actually mean. Indeed, each of the norms in the list must require positive legal statement to make clear what in fact would constitute a violation of the norm, how such a violation is to be dealt with, what penalty must follow, and what consequences there may be for the life of the society if the norm is flaunted by many within the society.

Already we can see the difference between such norms and what we call positive or negative laws. These are not laws in the ordinary sense of the term *law*. The Ten Commandments are much more akin to statements about the character of life in community than they are to cases of violation of the law of the community and what punishment is to be dealt out when the violations occur. Put in constitutional terms, the Ten Commandments are much more like the Bill of Rights and its amendments than the United States Code.[4] They provide the policy statements that can help a new member of the community come to clarity rather quickly regarding what is the shape of life within our community. They will not provide for that new community member all that is needed to guide his or her life legally. There have to be judges to settle particular cases and to render equal or comparably fair acts of judgment. And there must be collections of cases with which these judges may work.

THE VALUE OF NORMS IN CONTEMPORARY SOCIETY

It would appear that if some way could be found to make credible such fundamental norms for our common life, the whole society would benefit, not just the religious community. Certainly the widespread moral confusion that we see all around us and often feel within us could be eased. The fact that these were originally prohibitions, in quite short form, should also be kept in mind. Such prohibitions are particularly valuable because they leave open many matters that must be settled in other ways. For example, what is adultery? What does it mean to take God's name in vain? What would constitute a violation of the seventh day? What kinds of acts would show dishonor for one's parents? All such matters must be settled. The short, pithy prohibitions do not get into that kind of particularity. They simply let the community, and each individual within the community, know what kinds of human conduct are in principle ruled out, not allowable, not to be entertained at all.

And therein lies their great utility for our time. What is called "situation ethics" has done much to tie the decisions taken by individuals and groups to the concrete realities of given and changing situations and circumstances. Such an approach to ethics has enormous value. It requires moral agents to take stock of the actual situations, the actual potential gains and losses in a planned act. Its weakness is also evident: were all decisions to be taken in such a way, the moral energy of an individual or group would soon be exhausted. Much of the conduct of individuals and groups must be guided by flat prohibitions, of the "ten commandments" sort, that rule out actions that can be entertained and that may indeed be tempting but are in fact not to be taken—quite simply because such actions are not permitted to members of this particular community.

What are the kinds of conduct that, for many families and individuals in the "Christian" Western lands, are simply ruled out in this way? Apparently only acts of fundamental dishonesty and of violence against the neighbor. Christians may, it seems, be haters of Jews without confronting such a flat and uncompromising prohibition. They may treat blacks as less than equal to whites and not run up against such a prohibition. They may engage in acts of adultery in their community and, if not caught, apparently feel no sense of having violated a specific commandment. They may work seven days a week with a kind of frantic commitment to moneymaking and never have it enter their minds that such frenetic labor is a violation of the absolute prohibition against working all the time.

It may appear before we have finished our study that the Ten Commandments contain some prohibitions that are as important today as they ever were but that others of them have lost much if not all of their significance. I suspect, however, that we shall come to see that a restatement of the Ten Commandments without much change in their actual contents will show up as extremely powerful for our time and generation.

One thing is unmistakable: all too many of our fellow citizens, and we among them, find it very difficult indeed to gain guidance and moral strength from such summary statements as the Ten Commandments. We need such understandings very badly indeed. Our society needs such understandings. And the church needs them desperately as a part of its liturgical life, its teaching and interpretive activity, its counseling, and its prophetic pronouncements.

Such a set of prohibitions would need to avoid the temptation to be too concrete and specific in moral pronouncements, settling questions on the basis of abstract principles too quickly applied to particular cases. As we shall see, the Ten Commandments are not at all abstract, but they are not too specific with regard to particulars either. They are specifications of what kinds of conduct are ruled out in principle, but they retain their value and their capacity to guide us even when we violate them. Perhaps it is especially when we have violated one of the commandments that the moral weight of the commandment is at its height. We are not simply condemned and placed under judgment; we are shown to have engaged in conduct that is not permitted. We are simply not permitted to have sexual relations with a person other than our spouse in marriage, for example. If we do so, we know that we have done something not allowed. In that way we know where we stand.

Under contemporary conditions it is virtually impossible for young men and women to know what it is that the society, and especially the religious society, rules out in principle. Jewish youth are potentially better off than Christian youth, for in the Jewish tradition the idea of Torah as a set of guidelines for the common life is more nearly intact than it is within the Christian community. But I am told that the presence of a commitment to Torah on the part of young Jews can no longer be taken for granted either.

We shall have something to say below about how the community might proceed to keep such prohibitions up-to-date and vividly before the members of the community. Here I wish only to underscore the point that if it should prove possible to help ourselves and our fellow human beings recover the sense of the power of a set of prohibitions that simply must be observed because to fail to do so would be ruinous, we might begin to see a drop in the frightful anxieties that beset young men and women and their parents as well. How desperately some parents these days try to discover what they should teach their children morally! And how little guidance they get from church and synagogue!

I believe that if we did nothing more than reaffirm the importance of the Ten Commandments as such guidelines, with no interpretation of them at all—no updating, no clarification— we would provide help of a very welcome kind to such parents. The Ten Commandments do need interpretation and efforts to discern their hidden riches. But if the choice is the present state of affairs or a return to allegiance to this old collection quite uninterpreted, I would very much choose the latter situation. Even so, it is probably unwise to suggest that families or con- gregations *can* reinstate the Decalogue without interpretation. We have to attempt a restatement of its import and claim.

In the next chapter we will undertake to place this collection of ancient prohibitions in its historical and literary and cul- tural setting. We will try to trace the antecedents of the collec- tion in ancient Israel, and we will venture to suggest what the original Ten Commandments probably contained before addi- tions were made to the list. As we do so we will be able to test some of the declarations made in the present chapter, at least with regard to ancient Israel. We will see that the list with which we are dealing differs fundamentally from ancient ritual curses and from specific "statutes" forbidding certain crimes. The Ten Commandments have been called by a recent interpreter "An- cient Israel's Criminal Law."[5] That is precisely what they are *not*. The collection is a list in the form of a declaration. The tone is not so threatening as the tone of "the curses," and it is not even so weighty and ponderous as formally similar legal "statutes" that specify the death penalty for certain grave offenses. But the tone is also not rightly described as sermonic or hortatory. Some of the expansions of the commandments are hortatory, but the set of prohibitions is straightforward, laconic, unqualified, matter-of-course. God, the Lord of the covenant, has brought a band of slaves to freedom. Now the same God lays upon the freed slaves a set of obligations. The prohibitions are put in such form that they are not at all Israelite in content, even though they clearly are intended for the Israelite community. They flatly describe certain kinds of human behavior that are uncompromisingly eliminated; no one, no individual or family or group or whole people, is permitted to do such things. Ten in number, these prohibitions can be numbered on the ten fingers of the two hands and thus better remembered. Not all human conduct is thereby covered. And the commandments cry out for interpretation and will have to receive such interpretation.

One thing is unmistakable: the freed slaves are bound to God in a very special way by these ten prohibitions. God does not explain what consequences will follow upon the violation of the prohibitions. God does not warn or threaten. God simply commands, commands as the one who has shown grace and love in bringing a band of slaves to freedom. Israel as a people and each individual Israelite may disobey one or several or all these commandments. No threat is stated should that happen. But no Israelite needs to hear the threat. Each hearer of this list will know without being told that it is sheer folly and perhaps even madness to violate these requirements, for to do so cannot help but bring harm. These prohibitions are designed for the good of these freed slaves. Life and joy and peace lie ahead for those who quite simply rule out such conduct as is here specified. God has a right to demand what God will, and God does not need to explain.

How could such a collection have originated? Almost certainly, the contents were there deeply imbedded within parts of the community before anyone put together just these prohibitions. But I think it a work of genius, humanly viewed, that someone brought just these ten prohibitions together and set them forth for the community to accept, and in the strength of these prohibitions to find orientation for life. While Moses cannot certainly be said to be that person of genius, it would be surprising to discover that he had no hand in the production of the list. We shall look at that matter later on.

CHAPTER 2

The Origin, Structure,
and Setting of the
Ten Commandments

RECENT PERSPECTIVES

The Ten Commandments have received a great deal of attention in recent research. Commentaries on the Books of Exodus and Deuteronomy have brought together much of this research, as have several articles in dictionaries of the Bible recently published. In addition, many studies on the early traditions of Israel, on the development of law in Israel and in the ancient Near East, and on the history of Israel's worship and early institutional life have illuminated the place of the Ten Commandments in Israel's life and thought. While there has emerged no consensus on such matters as the precise origin and date of the Decalogue or on its relation to the Israelite cult, the alternative ways of understanding the Decalogue are today very clearly in focus.

The most thorough and imaginative study of the Ten Commandments recently undertaken is that by Eduard Nielsen, *The Ten Commandments in New Perspective.*[1] Much of what is found in Nielsen's book will find echoes in the following pages, although I disagree with him about the date and the early setting of the Ten Commandments as a whole and also am quite unpersuaded by several of his ideas (concerning the origin of the Sabbath, for example). Nielsen has worked carefully through problems of textual transmission, the form of the commandments, the history of the elaboration of the early form, and the overall import of the commandments for ancient Israel. His conclusion that the earliest form of a set of ten prohibitions, which he tentatively reconstructs, comes from the ninth century in North Israel seems to me unconvincing. I am not at all persuaded by his arguments that this early decalogue was promulgated by a North Israelite king as royal law. At the same time, Nielsen's thorough analysis of all issues and problems connected with the Decalogue is masterful.

Johann Jakob Stamm has devoted many years of research to the Decalogue. His work is summed up in *Der Dekalog im Lichte der neueren Forschung,* which has been supplemented by Maurice Edward Andrew and translated into English under the title *The Ten Commandments in Recent Research.*[2] Stamm concludes that the second half of the Decalogue has analogies in the literature of ancient Egypt and Mesopotamia but that the first four of the commandments are distinctive of Israelite religious understanding and strikingly different from the views of the neighboring peoples. These opening four commandments, plus the prologue, tie the demands laid upon the people to Yahweh's historical deliverance of the Israelites from Egypt. The requirements also belong to a great festive act of worship that commemorates the events of Israel's salvation.

Stamm concludes that it would be wrong to treat the Decalogue as law, to see it as some onerous burden laid upon the people by a stern and righteous judge. The Ten Commandments are rather to be seen as Israel's great charter of freedom. I agree entirely with this conclusion, although I am less confident than I was at one time regarding the connection of the Decalogue with Israel's early festival.

One of the highly influential recent studies of the Decalogue is that by Erhard Gerstenberger, *Wesen und Herkunft des "Apodiktischen Rechts,"*[3] which is presented as a refutation of the even more influential study of 1934 by Albrecht Alt, *The Origins of Israelite Law.*[4] Alt had maintained that the Ten Commandments were in form as well as content genuinely Israelite law, categorical in their statement of what Yahweh would not allow, depending upon regular recitation in connection with worship for their continuing authority in Israel. Gerstenberger pointed out that there are examples of categorical law in the ancient Near Eastern legal and wisdom materials that Alt had overlooked. Gerstenberger also shows that within the Israelite wisdom tradition there are collections of prohibitions akin to the provisions of the Decalogue. He concludes that it is best to locate the origin of the Ten Commandments in the moral instruction of the clans and the tribes of early Israel, rather than associate it with some distinct act in the life of Moses or in some great festival of early Israel.

It is correct that Alt's early study of Israelite law has to be modified. There were laws in the ancient Near Eastern world akin to those found in the Ten Commandments and in other legal collections of Israel. Formally, the Decalogue is not unique. But Gerstenberger has underestimated the significance of the Ten Commandments as a collection. He illuminates the question of where the Decalogue was used in the ongoing social life of the people, and he offers an important challenge and corrective to theories initiated by Alt that relate law perhaps too closely to the cultic life of early Israel. Gerstenberger offers no acceptable explanation to the formation of what is certainly a unique list of ten commandments (in its present form).

One of the most interesting and comprehensive short treatments of the Ten Commandments came from the work of George E. Mendenhall on ancient Near Eastern treaties.[5] This study of law and covenant, to which we will turn in more detail in the following paragraphs, has been a very positive and salutary step in research on ancient Near Eastern law. It now appears that the Decalogue may not fit into the form of the ancient Hittite treaty as well as Mendenhall had supposed. Even so, the analogy of the treaty between an overlord and a subject monarch or people is one that remains fruitful indeed as we attempt to locate the Decalogue in its setting at the dawn of Israelite history. This study of the treaty form has been elaborated and made more precise by Klaus Baltzer in his important book *The Covenant Formulary.*[6]

One recent study of the Ten Commandments seeks to identify the collection as precisely the text of ancient Israel's criminal law code. This work, by Anthony Phillips, is entitled *Ancient Israel's*

Criminal Law.[7] It is helpful in its comparisons of the provisions
of the Decalogue with other legal materials in Israel, and it is a
mine of information about particular legal practices and understandings, but it does little to illuminate the actual status and use
of the Ten Commandments. The resemblance between the Ten
Commandments and, for example, the Code of Hammurabi is so
slight, both formally and with regard to content, that I find it
inappropriate to speak of the Decalogue as a law code. And I
find the Decalogue to be a poor example even of a criminal code,
serving a more limited purpose than did the large collections of
laws in the ancient Near Eastern world.

Among the treatments of the Ten Commandments in recent
commentaries on the Book of Exodus or the Book of Deuteronomy, there are several of great value and helpfulness. The
commentary on Exodus by Brevard S. Childs[8] is the fullest of
recent ones, including also short treatments of the history of the
interpretation of the Decalogue in Jewish and Christian circles.
The exegetical study of the Decalogue by the late J. Philip Hyatt
is a model of clarity and succinct observation.[9] I shall depend
upon these two fine commentaries at quite a number of points.
Hyatt is more straightforward than Childs in attempting to give
a date for the "original" Ten Commandments. Childs is much
more interested in the basic meaning of the commandments for
the community of Israel in its central historical period than he
is in the connection of the Decalogue with Moses or with any
particular historical period. Such caution may be called for, but
one might wish that Childs had been more venturesome in identifying the probable original setting of the particular commandments and the collection as a whole.

As is the case in several areas of Old Testament scholarship
today, there is a movement toward dating the commandments
quite early, which is also paralleled by a movement in the opposite direction. No major writing has yet identified the Decalogue
as coming from the time of the Babylonian exile, as has been the
case, for example, with the traditions concerning Abraham.[10]
Such a view may be on the way. In the opposite direction, we

have the familiar inferences being drawn that since some arguments for a later dating of the Ten Commandments have shown up as unnecessary or unsatisfactory, Moses may well be the author. The discovery of the Ebla tablets may lead to new understandings of the origins of Israelite law. Whether that is the case or not, the discovery is already causing scholars to be wary of dating Israelite materials late. Even before the evidence is available for critical analysis, some interpreters are placing the early traditions of Israel much earlier than before. In this whole area the better approach is a cautious one. We do not yet know what effect the Ebla discoveries may have on our understandings of ancient Israel's legal materials. We have no reason to let the discoveries influence our attitude toward such matters, although it is difficult to avoid such influence.

ANCIENT NEAR EASTERN LEGAL MATERIALS

There are, however, many collections of laws from the ancient Near East and other legal or semilegal materials that we do know in some detail. These have been studied in relation to the Ten Commandments in many extremely important monographs, both those dealing with a single law collection or parts of it and those devoted to a more comprehensive examination of law in the ancient Near East in comparison with Israelite law. Basic to all such studies is the epoch-making work by Albrecht Alt, *The Origins of Israelite Law,* published in 1934.[11] Alt concluded that the characteristic form of Israelite law, as distinguished from ancient Oriental law in general, was its categorical or apodictic form, a form such as we find in the Ten Commandments as well as in other locations within the corpus of Israel's law. Alt judged at the time of his writing that such categorical law was without parallel in ancient Near Eastern societies outside Israel. That judgment is now known to have been in error.[12]

Alt also was convinced that the life-setting of the Decalogue was the early Israelite cult, and in particular the cultic recitation of the law at the old center of Shechem once every seventh year, as specified in Deut. 31:9–13. The Decalogue was thus Israel's covenant law, the community's absolute requirement from the God of the Covenant who had brought release from Egyptian bondage and had bound this people to himself in covenant. The original form of the commandments was a series of short, probably negative statements in the form of second-person singular verbal statements preceded by the strong negative particle *lō'*.

Other ancient Near Eastern legal materials do of course have their influence upon Israelite law. The second type of law that Alt identified he called case or casuistic law, law that in form often began with a general case, "If . . ." (or "When . . ."), and then indicated what the specific legal requirement was in the stated case. Such an opening case might then be further specified by the introduction of yet another subcase under the opening heading, with the use of a different Hebrew term. See Exod. 21:1–6 for a good listing of such casuistic law with its distinct provisions carefully set out.

The analogies between some of this case law and the ancient Near Eastern law codes are very close indeed. It is evident that either the early Israelites had access to some of these ancient collections of case law or there were similar collections developing at various locations in the ancient Near Eastern world. In my view, the early Israelites probably had access to such a collection that was being used by their neighbors in Canaan, perhaps before the time of Moses as well as following Moses' death. There surely must have been at least loose connections among the various cultures of the ancient Near Eastern world, for the law collections of the various countries do show remarkable similarities.[13] It is also possible, of course, that the early Israelites developed their categorical law, law like that in the Ten Commandments, in dependence upon the neighbors as well. But nowhere in the ancient Near Eastern world do we find anything like the *collection* of commandments that appears in our Decalogue. Even the parallels to the moral prohibitions or prescriptions of the Ten Commandments that show up in the Egyptian Coffin Texts, the Book of the Dead, and so on, are not a part of such a well-rounded, succinct collection.[14] The Egyptian parallels are usually in the form of specifications that the one laid to rest in death did not violate the specified prohibitions during the course of his lifetime.

CATEGORICAL LAW IN THE ANCIENT
NEAR EAST AND IN ISRAEL

We now will look briefly at some of these examples of categorical law in the literatures outside the Hebrew Bible. Two points will emerge, as indicated above: First, there are indeed analogies to the absolute prohibition of certain kinds of action, specified in the name of the High God. Second, there is no example of an extended collection of such prohibitions outside the Hebrew Bible.

Three areas of literature and thought contain the large number of currently recognized parallels to Israel's categorical law: ancient Near Eastern treaties; the Egyptian texts found in the coffins of the dead and in the so-called Book of the Dead, as well as in other similar literature; and some of the wisdom or wisdom-related texts of the ancient world.

Regarding the treaties, Dennis J. McCarthy[15] has worked the materials over with great care and has shown that there are indeed several good parallels to the categorical legal statements of the Hebrew Bible. These occur in treaties between equals but even more characteristically in treaties between an overlord and his vassals. The categorical provisions are frequently a part of the oath that the vassal swears, the contents of which are written down in the treaties: that one will not forget one's obligation to the overlord or to his successors; that one will not interfere with the household of the sovereign, upset the rules of succession laid down, or the like. Also noteworthy is the fact that in these treaties we have lists of specific cases intermingled with the categorical prohibitions or commandments. The sharp distinction drawn between the two types of law is not found in these treaties. See the appendix to McCarthy's work for good examples.

In the Book of the Dead we have lists of moral offenses of which the dead person, in texts prepared beforehand and highly stylized in the ritual provisions for the dead, protests innocence of particular crimes that are a part of the social and personal moral existence of any people. In some of the regular wisdom collections in Egypt, moreover, we also find commandments of an apodictic sort, and prohibitions as well. Gerstenberger looks in particular at the Wisdom of Amenemope for several examples.[16] Some Babylonian wisdom texts are also drawn upon, and then the wisdom texts from the Hebrew Bible itself are called forth to show that Israel used the categorical form in its wisdom tradition, in literature that derives from the clan and tribe ethos and spreads out from there to find a place in the court wisdom and in the wisdom schools of a later time.

Several studies of the forms of legal address have helped to make more precise distinctions among the various legal forms.[17] It has been shown, for example, that there are quite a few short rows of prohibitions that are introduced normally by the negative particle *lō',* and these are not by any means to be related exclusively to the absolute demands of Yahweh. The thesis of Gerstenberger has been modified and to some extent confirmed through such studies: There are indeed many different forms of prohibitions to be found in the literature of ancient Israel, and many of them have their seat in the clan ethos of early Israelite times, with parallels in the literatures and cultures of the ancient Near Eastern world. But it has also been shown that there is a rather close connection between the absolute prohibitions and the use of the terms *hoq* and *haqaq,* thus supporting the notion that there are two basic types of law in ancient Israel: the laws governing particular legal situations that must be decided upon on the basis of precedents—the *mishpaṭim*—which do have a distinct form of "when, and if, . . . then," and the type that is unconditional and in the second-person singular.[18] Albrecht Alt's fine study has been much modified as a result of later research, but this basic distinction drawn by Alt has been shown to be quite appropriate and sound by several of the more recent studies.

THE CURSE RITUAL OF DEUTERONOMY 27

We now raise the question whether there is any way to trace the probable origin of the Ten Commandments from similar materials preserved in the Old Testament itself. One of the most likely candidates has been preserved in the closing chapters of the Book of Deuteronomy. There must be some connection between Deut. 27:15–26 and the Decalogue.

A curse ritual like that in the Deuteronomy passage is unmistakably a cultic act, even if it is hardly possible to reconstruct completely this cultic act from the passages now scattered throughout the Books of Deuteronomy and Joshua (see in addition to Deut. 27:15–26: Deut. 11:26–32, Josh. 8:30–35, and Joshua 24). Most scholars grant that the curse ritual of Deuteronomy 27 is very old indeed, even though much-expanded literarily over the centuries.

Curses are a fixed part of the treaties of the ancient Near Eastern world. They are among the most important ways ancient peoples sought to secure the beneficent power of the gods for their society and to avert the malevolent powers. Curses have as their counterpart a series of blessings, but the curses are certainly the more important daily realities in the life of a people in the ancient Near East.[19]

Curses belong to everyday life, to the clan and tribe ethos as well as to particularly solemn cultic acts.[20] The series of curses in Genesis 3 (vv. 14–19) already shows the significance of the curse for ancient Israel. The speaking of words of power in a solemn setting, often accompanied by symbolic acts and gestures, puts the power of the words into effect. The curse depends for its efficacy upon the power of human speech as such, and especially upon the power of human address in special situations of life. The words of the curse, when spoken rightly and with the full force that is potentially theirs, go forth to accomplish the threat that they contain, not automatically but almost inevitably. Curse words can be averted by countervailing words.

The self-curse is a particular form of cursing. One takes upon oneself an oath that one will not do a certain kind of thing, or that one will do so, and then underscores the commitment by a solemn curse. This is just the purpose of the oaths in the treaties; the parties to the treaty bind themselves to observe its terms, and they invoke against themselves the power of the gods, the powers of the natural order, and indeed the human agencies and partners to the treaty, should they fail to live up to their commitments.[21]

Stanley Gevirtz has shown that in West Semitic curses from a wide variety of literatures and cultures we have something like our Ten Commandments, our categorical law.[22] And McCarthy, as noted above, has demonstrated just how widespread was the categorical command or prohibition within the ancient Near Eastern treaties.[23] Thus, the curse ritual with which we are here dealing is a part of literary and legal materials from the ancient world that have a particular closeness to the form of the Decalogue.

How near are the analogies of form and content with our Ten Commandments? The number ten seems not to occur. There are twelve tribes of Israel, and there is apparently intended to be a use of the number twelve to correspond with the number of the tribes or tribal representatives present for the ceremony. A division of the tribes into two parts may or may not be a part of the original cultic rite; I suspect that it is original and that the scene described is in fact a scene occasionally used in early, probably pre-Mosaic, times between the mountains Ebal and Gerizim near the ancient city of Shechem. The important thing, however, is not that certain tribes pronounced the blessings and others the curses; that is late elaboration and in principle not cultically satisfactory. Nor is any significance to be attached to which tribes stand to the north and which to the south. The basic cultic reality, in all likelihood, is a self-cursing ceremony in which leaders of the twelve tribes of Israel listen to the Levitical leaders pronounce curses upon any member of the tribal association that does one of the prohibited acts, and all the assembled group responds with "Amen," thereby taking upon themselves the curse words and their effects, recognizing that the doing of such deeds will bring into play, almost automatically, this curse that now hovers over them.[24]

Such curses would then be recited in the settlements of the individual tribes and would be committed to memory by those responsible for leadership within the tribes. In this way, the contents of the curses would have become a part of the ethos of the tribe, within which all members would live out their lives. The regular gatherings for the recitation of the curses would have done much to make vivid and powerful these words of cursing, but not everything would have depended upon such cultic recitations.

It is evident, therefore, that we would be unwise to choose between supposed sharp alternatives: cultic setting versus family or clan ethos. The one can reinforce the power of the other. The occurrence of the phrase "do wanton folly in Israel," which would appear to be closely tied to the curse ritual and the world from which it comes, supports the connection between cultic recitation of curses and the daily situations of the common life.[25] People in ancient Israel knew that the contents of these curses were to be observed, on peril of death that one had in fact invited. The process thus seems to be one in which, first, the family and clan ethos provided the setting for the new members of the community to come to consciousness regarding what Yahweh would not allow and what were the basic requirements of life in this community. Next, these would have been underscored and given a weighty and threatening status through the religious rites and practices of the community or the larger tribal or intertribal entities. Chief among these rites would have been a curse ritual such as we have in Deuteronomy 27. Then this ritual self-cursing becomes a binding oath of the people, through its own representatives to the sacred center where the ritual is recited, that will be committed to memory, talked about, and made into one of the regular instruments of policy out of which the decisions of the elders would come. The self-cursings remain religious rites, but they arise out of the family ethos, sum it up, and in turn contribute to the deepening and the making specific of the family or clan moral directives.

Formally, the curses have a quite regular set of expressions. The passive participle of one of the common verbs for cursing is used, probably in order to avoid the suggestion that Yahweh himself directly brings the curses upon the people in an automatic, mechanical way. "Cursed be the one who . . ." is a very common way of dealing with the curse, as has been shown by

Gevirtz.[26] It is theologically and cultically safer to speak that way than to say "Yahweh curse you!" Indeed, the same care is observed in the pronouncing of blessings, not because blessings are dangerous but because blessings are the regular counterpart of the very dangerous cursings. We know that within the passive form of speech there lurks a double meaning: "May anyone be cursed who dares to do X or Y" and "Anyone who dares to do X or Y is thereby accursed." The same applies to blessings, for the power of human speech to effect blessing or cursing is already there in the act of speaking, to some degree. One is in a position to effect blessing, not simply to pray for it; and the same is true of the pronouncement of cursing. Even so, the delicacy of the use of the passive participle that leaves the origin of the curse somewhat vague and indefinite is unmistakable.

The passive participle is followed by an active participle, which in turn is followed by the object, describing the one against whom the proscribed deed is done. As mentioned above, the form is quite regular, and it may be possible to make the form even more regular by very slight modifications of the received text. Our reconstruction of the original curse ritual follows:

Deut. 27:15   Cursed is the one who makes a graven or a molten image.

27:16   Cursed is the one who treats his father or mother with contempt.

27:17   Cursed is the one who removes the landmark of his neighbor.

27:18   Cursed is the one who leads a blind person astray.

27:19   Cursed is the one who turns aside the justice due the sojourner.

27:20   Cursed is the one who sleeps with the wife of his father.

27:21   Cursed is the one who sleeps with any animal.

27:22   Cursed is the one who sleeps with his sister.

27:23   Cursed is the one who sleeps with his mother-in-law.

27:24   Cursed is the one who strikes his neighbor in secret.

27:25   Cursed is the one who takes a bribe.

27:26   Cursed is the one who treats with contempt the words of this teaching.

One could make a decalogue of the curse ritual by eliminating the first of the prohibitions, since it would appear to belong in the realm of the religious and the cultic, and by eliminating the last of the curses, since it is so general. The last of the curses is general, and it also seems to have been augmented editorially to a greater extent than the other curses, as our reconstruction above would indicate. The first curse, against anyone who makes an image, is different in kind from the others, but we think it belongs with the list. The making of an image of the deity, whether of Yahweh or of some other god, was looked upon as the same kind of abhorrent act, worthy of immediate death, as lying with one's mother. I am persuaded, therefore, that we have a list that originally included twelve curses, the number itself being arrived at on the basis of the long-standing tradition that Israel consisted of the descendants of the twelve sons of the patriarch Jacob.

Much of the description found in Deuteronomy 27 may be late and fictitious. I sought years ago to reconstruct the original curse-scene from the time of Joshua and perhaps from an earlier period as well.[27] Assuming a regular fall ceremony of the New Year, which became for the early Israelites an occasion for the reaffirmation of the covenant bond between them and Yahweh, we can suppose that the representatives of the "twelve" tribes would gather at Shechem for the reaffirmation of the covenant and for the pledging of their continuing allegiance to one another in the federation of the tribes as well as to Yahweh. The curse ritual would have been the closing ceremony on this occasion: After the proceedings in the Shechem region, beside the sacred oak tree and at the site of memorial stones, the representatives would have marched in procession to the west and taken their position in two half circles between the mountains Ebal and

Gerizim. The Levites would have stood between the divided groups, divided in such fashion as to provide representatives of six tribes facing Ebal and six tribal representatives facing Gerizim. The Levites would have pronounced the curses, and the group as a whole would have shouted the "Amen!" placing upon themselves and the folk at home whom they represented the power of these curses. The division of the people into two parts may have been a symbolic reenactment of ancient oath ceremonies connected with covenant-making of the sort that we can see reflected in Gen. 15:7–21. The two parts of the people represent the divided animals whose dismembered parts were once set over against one another as a sign that they too were to suffer the fate of such animals if they proved unfaithful to the covenant they had made.

With regard to the contents of the curse list, there is not a great deal of resemblance to the Ten Commandments, at least not at first glance. Our curse ritual is concerned especially with those acts of a people that can be done in secret, those that only God can easily mark and see. They are a reminder to the people that God in fact does see and take note of their misdeeds, and that they should not suppose otherwise. The Ten Commandments, on the other hand, are designed to cover a range and variety of human conduct both within the larger community of Israel and within the family circle, indeed, within the very interior workings of the passions of the individual. The correspondence that we do observe, therefore, may be considerable, given the different purposes that the two lists have.

The following table indicates that the two lists do have a good deal in common, although there is little likelihood that the Ten Commandments simply emerged from such curse rituals as the one we have in Deuteronomy 27.

Curse Ritual of Deuteronomy 27:15–26	Ten Commandments of Exodus 20:2–17
27:15 Curse on making of images	20:4–6 Prohibition of images

27:16 Curse on the one treating parents with contempt	20:12 Command to honor parents (perhaps originally in negative form; see below)
27:17 Curse on the one who removes the neighbor's landmark	20:15 Prohibition of theft
27:18 Curse on leading the blind astray	20:15 (?) Prohibition of theft
27:19 Curse on the one turning aside the justice due the neighbor	20:16 Prohibition of bearing false witness
27:20–23 Curse on the one involved in incest or bestiality	20:14 Prohibition of adultery
27:24 Curse on the one who strikes the neighbor secretly	20:13 Prohibition of killing
27:25 Curse on the one taking a bribe	20:16 Prohibition of bearing false witness
27:26 Curse on the one treating this teaching with contempt	20:3 (?) Worship of God alone

We can see readily that the Ten Commandments represent a more comprehensive and more general list. The curse ritual, nonetheless, may well have provided some impetus to the creation of the Ten Commandments. Before we attempt to identify just what impetus it provided, we should look at other lists of ten or twelve commandments, prohibitions, or curses. Are there other analogies to the Ten Commandments in form and number?

OTHER "DECALOGUES"

There are indeed other lists of commandments or prohibitions, frequently mixed listings of prohibitions and positive com-

mands, as in the present Ten Commandments. The closest
analogy to the Ten Commandments is found in Exod. 34:14–26,
a list of prescriptions largely concerned with the observance of
the feasts of Israel and of rites connected with that observance.
Twelve commandments can be identified:

1. The worship of no other God (v. 14)
2. No molten gods (v. 17)
3. Observance of the feast of unleavened bread (v. 18)
4. Offering Yahweh all that opens the womb (vv. 19–20)
5. Sabbath observance (v. 21)
6. Observance of the feast of weeks (v. 22)
7. Observance of the feast of ingathering at the year's end
    (v. 22)
8. Males to appear before Yahweh three times in the year
    (v. 23)
9. No use of leaven in the sacrifices (v. 25)
10. None of Passover sacrifice to be left until morning (v.
    25)
11. First of the first fruits to be brought to the Lord's house
    (v. 26)
12. No boiling of a kid in the milk of its mother (v. 26)[28]

Of these, scholars have been able to eliminate the fifth and
the eighth, since Sabbath observance hardly seems to belong to
this list of largely cultic observances and since the reference to
the appearance before Yahweh three times in the year is adequately covered by the reference to the individual feasts of unleavened bread and weeks and ingatherings. Such elimination
provides a decalogue that would appear to be concerned with
the regulation of sacred time and sacred rites of a sort we might
suppose was characteristic of Israel early in her life in the land
of Canaan. Thus, the "ritual decalogue" has often been said to
belong to the period prior to the "ethical decalogue," both of
them lying in time later than the time of Moses.

Nielsen wishes to associate the ritual decalogue with the reform of Josiah and to maintain that it is just then when the need
to specify a set of ritual and cultic requirements might have been

felt most keenly by the reformers in Josiah's day.[29] This view may well be right. In any case, there is no reason to date the "ethical decalogue" later than the "ritual decalogue" on the basis of some notion of how the religion of ancient Israel evolved. Such notions of historical evolution are entirely too subjective to be of assistance.

Another candidate for the status of decalogue occurs in Lev. 18:6–18, although in this list there are more problems in identifying our dodecalogue or decalogue. Here is the list as reconstructed by some:

1. General prohibition: Do not approach sexually anyone who is near of kin (v. 6).
2. Do not uncover the nakedness of your father, namely your mother (v. 7).
3. Nor your father's wife (one's own stepmother) (v. 8).
4. Nor your sister, either the daughter of your father or of your mother (v. 9).
5. Thought to be missing from original list: Nor your daughter (added between v. 9 and v. 10).
6. Nor your son's daughter or daughter's daughter (i.e., your granddaughter) (v. 10).
7. Nor your father's wife's daughter begotten of your father (v. 11).
8. Father's sister (v. 12).
9. Mother's sister (v. 13).
10. Father's brother (i.e., father's brother's wife) (v. 14).
11. Daughter-in-law (v. 15).
12. Brother's wife (i.e., sister-in-law) (v. 16).
13. Nor a woman and her daughter (v. 17).
14. Nor a woman as a rival wife to her sister (v. 18).[30]

Again we can eliminate some of these without too great difficulty. The first is a general prohibition and probably does not belong in the original list. Second, we have a duplicate in number 7 (v. 11), where sexual relations with one's sister are again prohibited (see number 4, v. 9). The thirteenth and fourteenth also belong to a different set of prohibitions, or at least to a slightly different perspective on sexual offenses, and may perhaps be eliminated from the originally narrow list of such offenses against members of one's own family.

That elimination leaves a decalogue of sexual prohibitions, very probably on the analogy of our own Ten Commandments as to number, and with the list made to make up originally this number of ten. We do not learn anything about the origin of the number ten from a study of this list of cultic prohibitions. And it does not seem, as a list, to be nearly as old as the cultic specifications of the curse ritual of Deuteronomy 27 dealing partially with the same subject.

One other possible decalogue appears in the Book of Leviticus. Chapter 20, beginning at v. 2, describes a number of crimes and specifies the penalty for their perpetrators. The list is as follows:

1. Giving of children to Molech (child sacrifice?) (vv. 2–5)
2. Consulting mediums and wizards (vv. 6–7)
3. Cursing father or mother (vv. 8–9)
4. Adultery with the wife of one's neighbor (v. 10)
5. Lying with one's father's wife (v. 11)
6. Lying with one's daughter-in-law (v. 12)
7. Lying with another male (v. 13)
8. Lying with one's wife and with the wife's mother (v. 14)
9. Lying with a beast (v. 15)
10. A woman's lying with a beast (v. 16)

The list continues, but the crimes forbidden are of a somewhat different sort, being a bit further beyond the immediate family situation and also not involving explicitly the death penalty, as in the cases enumerated. It is noteworthy, however, that sexual relations with the sister are forbidden in v. 17, a crime that might well have been a part of the original "decalogue" and that certainly would normally carry the death penalty as well.

We should look briefly at two other such lists, one from the Book of Psalms and the other from the Book of Ezekiel. The Ezekiel list, which appears in slightly varying form three times in chapter 18, is a list of crimes that one is not to commit, identified by interpreters as a negative confession, a specification of offenses of which one is not guilty. The list from Ezek. 18:5–9 is partly negative and partly positive. It reads:

1. One who does not eat upon the mountains (v. 6)
2. Does not lift up his eyes to idols (v. 6)
3. Does not defile his neighbor's wife (v. 6)
4. Does not approach a woman in her time of impurity (v. 6)
5. Does not oppress anyone, but restores to the debtor his pledge (v. 7)
6. Does not commit robbery (v. 7)
7. Does give bread to the hungry (v. 7)
8. Does cover the naked with a garment (v. 7)
9. Does not lend at interest (v. 8)
10. Does not take an increase (v. 8)
11. Does withhold hand from iniquity (v. 8)
12. Does execute true justice between man and man (v. 8)
13. Does walk in God's statutes and observe his ordinances (v. 9)

The variations found in the later summations (vv. 10–13 and 14–17) seem to support the view that the prophet Ezekiel is simply listing a set of positive requirements and prohibitions numbering approximately ten, and probably using a list that was already available to him and widely employed in cultic practices designed to enable worshipers to declare themselves to be righteous before God, able to participate cultically in the worship of Yahweh, and committed to the cause of Yahweh.

With regard to the number ten, it seems best to cut the list off after number eleven above and place numbers nine and ten together, because there is no way to distinguish sharply between lending at interest and taking an increase. The renumbered tenth commandment, "withholds his hand from iniquity," would then be a general one, rounding off the list of things required of or prohibited to the righteous person.[31]

The parallel to the Ten Commandments found in the Psalms, pointed out many years ago by Sigmund Mowinckel,[32] occurs in Psalm 15. In vv. 2 through 5 of this psalm, identified as connected with the entrance of the community through the gates of the temple precincts in solemn procession on the high holy days (see also Psalm 24), we have another list of those qualities that mark the righteous person, negatively and positively:

1. Walks blamelessly and does what is right
2. Speaks truth from his heart
3. Does not slander with his tongue
4. Does no evil to his friend
5. Does not take up a reproach against his neighbor
6. In whose eyes a reprobate one is despised
7. Honors those who fear the Lord
8. Swears to his own hurt and does not change his testimony
9. Does not put out his money at interest
10. Does not take a bribe against the innocent

The list once more seems to aim at reaching the number ten, and probably for the same reasons that gave rise to our Ten Commandments, so far as the number is concerned—namely, to make the commandments and prohibitions easily remembered. But the setting in life of the lists in Ezekiel 18 and the list found here (with a much abbreviated one in Psalm 24) is quite different, clearly, from that of the lists in the Books of Exodus and Leviticus.[33]

We can see this difference in setting from the context of the several lists, but it also shows up with regard to the form of the lists themselves. Note the following formal characteristics of the lists:

In Exod. 34:14–26, the first form to occur is the negative particle *lō'* plus the second-person singular imperfect verb followed by the object. "You shall worship no other God" is the prohibition, as we saw (34:14). The negative form appears in v. 17 also, but it is preceded by the object. Of the remaining ten commandments in the full list of twelve, all but three are positive commandments (the negative ones being numbers nine, ten, and twelve). But the second-person singular form of the verb is regularly used.

In Lev. 18:6–18 we find a quite regular form. The object is

stated first ("The nakedness of X . . .") and then follows the negative particle *lō'* plus the second-person singular imperfect form of the verb. Thereafter, brief explanatory words may appear. Neither of these first two lists of commandments contains a statement of punishments to be exacted upon violaters of the commandments. In Lev. 20:2–16(17), the forms vary considerably. One commonly occurring form in the list is "Anyone who does . . . [third-person singular imperfect verb, preceded by the term *'ish 'asher*], dying he shall die [*mōt yūmat*]." In every instance the punishment for the crime is the death penalty (through v. 16).

Ezekiel 18:5–9 and Psalm 15 simply list very briefly the positive acts that indicate the righteousness of the person or the negative acts, avoidance of which testifies to the person's righteousness. These lists are "confessional mirrors," as they have been called, holding before the community and its individual members the qualities of life that Yahweh approves and insists upon within the community that approaches him as Lord.[34] They are not "laws" in the sense that the lists from Exodus and Leviticus are.

Of the five lists, the first two (Exod. 34:14–26 and Lev. 18:6–18) clearly resemble more nearly the form of the Ten Commandments. But neither of these two lists is at all close to the *contents* of the Decalogue. Closer to the contents of the Decalogue is the old curse ritual of Deut. 27:15–26. It is very difficult indeed, however, to see how our Decalogue could actually have been derived from the curse ritual, as we saw above.

Is this study of other "decalogues" actually a help in identifying the origin of the Decalogue or of its place in early Israelite society? It is of considerable importance, I believe. There are too many lists, with too many similarities to the Decalogue, for such lists to be accidental. I believe that the Ten Commandments served as the paradigm for most of them (excluding the curse ritual of Deuteronomy 27). The formation of this distinctive set of prohibitions in early Israelite life probably created a disposition to collect such short, pithy lists as we have been examining. Some of the latter served particular purposes in the literary traditions to which they belong. None of them, however, is likely to have had the influence that the Decalogue had, an influence that can be seen in *all* the traditions of early Israel—in the Psalms, in the prophetic traditions, in the wisdom traditions, in the narratives, and in later, intertestamental literatures. Our effort to examine several lists akin to the Decalogue has revealed a part of that influence of the Decalogue upon subsequent tradition. The influence goes much further and requires a study in itself.

THE "ORIGINAL" FORM OF THE TEN COMMANDMENTS

If we start with the assumption that the Ten Commandments consisted originally of ten short sentence-statements, most of them negative, we can best "restore" the "original" form of the Decalogue by simply lopping off the parts that seem clearly to be explanatory or unnecessary additions to the short, "original" form. Doing so, we have a set of commandments in the following form:

1. There shall not be to thee other gods before me.
2. Thou shalt not make for thyself a graven image.
3. Thou shalt not lift up the name of the Lord thy God for mischief.
4. Remember the sabbath day to sanctify it.
5. Honor thy father and thy mother.
6. Thou shalt not kill.
7. Thou shalt not commit adultery.
8. Thou shalt not steal.
9. Thou shalt not answer thy neighbor as a false witness.
10. Thou shalt not covet the household of thy neighbor.

The question is, however, whether we cannot come closer to the "original" form of the commandments than by the mere expedient of shortening the present sentences. Eduard Nielsen has reviewed efforts of scholars to do so and has proposed a reconstruction of his own that is quite impressive. Nielsen restores the commandments to short sentences, each of which has a direct object of the verb, and all the verbs being in the second-person singular form preceded by the negative particle *lō'*. His translation is as follows:[35]

1. Thou shalt not bow down before any other god.
2. Thou shalt not make to thyself any idol.
3. Thou shalt not take the name of Yahweh in vain.
4. Thou shalt not do any work on the sabbath day.
5. Thou shalt not despise thy father or thy mother.
6. Thou shalt not commit adultery with thy neighbor's wife.
7. Thou shalt not pour out the blood of thy neighbor.
8. Thou shalt not steal any man from thy neighbor.
9. Thou shalt not bear false witness against thy neighbor.
10. Thou shalt not covet thy neighbor's house.

It should be noted that Nielsen has followed the idea of several scholars in making the eighth commandment refer to the stealing of a man, with the tenth commandment taking the place of the eighth in covering all acts of coveting, planning to take the goods of another, and doing so.[36] Nielsen also followed one of the old traditions for ordering the commandments by placing the commandment against adultery ahead of that against killing.

His reconstruction also benefits from comparative work with several of the commandments found in the Book of the Covenant (Exod. 20:23—23:33), as he seeks to decide just what the form of these sentence commands should be and what is the most likely contents for each. It is an excellent reconstruction, and what follows may well not be an improvement upon it at all. Nevertheless, all of us must share our best understandings.

I propose to retain the traditional order of the commandments and thus not reverse the position of the commandments against killing and adultery. I also believe that Nielsen has needlessly modified the first commandment. It makes good sense in its present form, and it can simply be shortened to read, "There shall not be for thee other gods." For the fourth commandment, I think that the negative form was "Thou shalt not treat with contempt the sabbath day." The fifth in its negative form I would restore as "Thou shalt not curse thy father or thy mother." The commandment against killing or murder I would simply have read "Thou shalt not kill thy neighbor," or perhaps in English translation it would be more elegant to translate, "Thou shalt not take the life of thy neighbor."

My reconstruction, then, is close to that of Nielsen but different in several respects. It reads as follows in English:[37]

1. There shall not be to thee (or: Thou shalt not have) other gods.
2. Thou shalt not make for thyself an idol.
3. Thou shalt not lift up the name of Yahweh for mischief.
4. Thou shalt not despise (or treat with contempt) the sabbath day.
5. Thou shalt not curse thy father or thy mother.
6. Thou shalt not kill (or take the life of) thy neighbor.
7. Thou shalt not commit adultery with the wife of thy neighbor.
8. Thou shalt not steal anything that is thy neighbor's.
9. Thou shalt not answer thy neighbor as a false witness.
10. Thou shalt not covet the household of thy neighbor.

MOSES THE AUTHOR?

When we examine the contents of these short prohibitions as reconstructed above, we can see that there is no objection in principle to attributing them to the time of Moses, under certain presuppositions. If it be supposed, as I believe, that Moses did bring a band (perhaps a small band) of slaves from servitude in Egypt, guided them through the wilderness for some years, and worked out with them a set of guidelines for their existence resting basically upon the exclusive claim of the God who had delivered them from slavery upon the whole of their lives, then the contents of the commandments, although striking, are certainly in keeping with such an understanding of God.

We shall need to look at the individual commandments before we come to conclusions regarding whether any of them arose at a later time. For the present, I see no objection to assigning the contents of any one of the commandments to Moses. The contents of most of them, indeed, can fit many different cultures and periods of time and have analogies in many of the cultures of the ancient Near East. It is another question whether the row of commandments as a whole, as a series of ten commandments in negative form that still do not carry any penalties against those who violate them and do not have the "feel" of the curses of Deuteronomy 27, would be likely to have originated with Moses. We have seen that the idea of a treaty covenant made between Moses and the people, in Yahweh's name, does not find any normal or obvious expression in this list of brief prohibitions. In my judgment, the Ten Commandments as a series are from Moses. They are a remarkable discovery of this founder of Israelite religion, and they underlie and sum up the very heart and center of Israel's religion. It will be the task of the following chapters to make this contention a plausible one and to show the basis upon which it rests.

THE SETTING

A further difficulty must be noted: the setting of the Ten Commandments. Chapters 19–24 and 32–34 of the Book of Exodus are among the most complicated chapters in the Bible to analyze as to the development of the traditions they contain. J. Philip Hyatt has an illuminating treatment, giving his judgment as to the literary strata of the chapters and showing the view of many critics of how the documents or traditions "J" and "E" and "D" are to be separated and how we are to account for the present arrangement of the material.[38]

For our purposes the important thing is to try to understand how the Ten Commandments were placed into their present literary context and why they were so placed. We may begin by noting that chapter 19, very much worked over by the Deuteronomistic historian (the person responsible for revising and bringing together the Book of Deuteronomy and the present form of Joshua, Judges, 1 and 2 Samuel, and 1 and 2 Kings, and for making modest changes in Genesis, Exodus, Leviticus, and Numbers), seems to continue in Exod. 20:18–21, as Hyatt points out. In Exod. 20:22–26 there is old cultic material that may belong as the introductory part to the Book of the Covenant or the Covenant Code (Exodus 21–23). In any case, they do not represent any continuation of the narrative of 20:18–21, nor do they contain laws of the sort found in the Ten Commandments.

The opening verse of Exodus 20 is a very short (deliberately short?) introduction to the Ten Commandments themselves. Is it possible to discover why anyone would have wished to place the Ten Commandments here, between Exod. 19:25 and 20:18? In all likelihood, the Ten Commandments were located here on the basis of the simple fact that 19:25 contains a reference to Moses' telling the people of God's directions to him. This inadvertent mislocation of the Ten Commandments is therefore not important. But where did they appear earlier? Where was the traditional location of the Ten Commandments within the context of the stories of Moses and the people at Sinai?

Presently available evidence does not give us an answer. If it were certain that the materials of the Ten Commandments were modeled upon an ancient Near Eastern treaty, then we might be content with saying that the only needed context would be the narrative telling of the Israelites' arrival at Sinai and of Moses' receiving from the sovereign Yahweh the contents of the treaty stipulations. If, however, we must instead say that several elements of Exodus 19–24 and Exodus 32–34 remind us of the treaty form, but that there is not preserved for us any real example of the Hittite or ancient Near Eastern treaty form in these chapters (name and titles of the sovereign, historical prologue telling of past relations between the two countries, the stipulations of the treaty, call for the placing of copies of the treaty in temples and for its periodic reading within both lands, list of witnesses, including the names of gods as witnesses, and a list of blessings and cursings), then the location of the Ten Commandments within the various contexts of Exodus 19–24 would appear to be arbitrary, wherever it was placed. Our best analogy for the order of the elements (apart from the entire Book of Deuteronomy itself) in the treaties is Joshua 24. There we have the historical prologue, various hortatory stipulations, a reference to the making of a covenant and to the presentation of statutes and ordinances. Reference to the stone as a witness, the location of the curse ritual of Deuteronomy 27 and the blessings and cursings of Deuteronomy 28, and their relation to the site of Shechem (see Josh. 8:30–34 and Deut. 11:26–30) might enable us to reconstruct such a covenant ritual, but even then the reconstruction is from portions of the Torah and of Joshua that by no means are now set forth together.[39]

Thus we are driven back to the point that if there is reason for assigning the Ten Commandments to the time of Moses we are not able to restore the account of their presentation by Moses to the people. These chapters have been worked over too much by the later generations. No longer is it possible to reconstruct from them the kind of setting within which such a disclosure of God's requirements of his freed slaves probably arose.

If we simply speculate, we might well conclude that the tradition has preserved for us a reasonable account. The people are brought by Moses to the very mountain of revelation on the basis of which he was led to return to Egypt and lead the slaves to freedom. At this sacred mountain the people commit themselves to the worship of Yahweh, identified by Moses as the God of their forebears (see Exodus 3 and 6). They spend some time in the valley at the base of this mountain, while Moses continues his work to shape for them a form of organization and a set of requirements that will hold them together as a people. One of the essential elements of the requirements is the Ten Commandments in their short form, approximately as reconstructed above. The people leave the holy mountain to continue their journey to the land of the promise. They leave as God's people, with the essential terms of their relation to God summed up in a series of ten short, pithy sentence-prohibitions.

NUMBERING THE COMMANDMENTS

One other matter requires attention before we turn to the discussion of the individual commandments. While there has been unanimity, until recent times, in the identification of ten commandments—no more and no fewer—there has been far from complete agreement as to which of the commandments in fact make up the list of ten. Some have included the prefatory statement that identifies God the Lord as the one who brought the Israelites from Egyptian bondage and who now lays upon them the commandments, making this introduction into the first of the commandments. While there is sound theological reasoning in such an enumeration, it does not seem to be the best listing of the ten commandments in an original, short list. We noted above that the commandment against adultery has occasionally been placed ahead of that against killing. But apart from that variation in the order (plus the listing of the wife instead of the household in Deut. 5:21 as over against Exod. 20:17), the material comprising the Decalogue follows a fixed order.

The other occasions for variations in the numbering center upon the commandments against the worship of other gods and against idolatry, which are sometimes taken as a single commandment and sometimes treated as two separate ones, and the commandment against coveting the neighbor's household (or wife, listed first in Deut. 5:21), which occasionally is divided into two separate commandments, with the house listed first (or the wife) as the ninth commandment and the other objects listed next as the tenth commandment. The following chart should be of help in identifying which of the methods of enumeration has the greatest plausibility. It should at the least assist the reader in avoiding confusion as to which commandments are referred to in the different religious communities.

The problems that led to the above disagreements appear to have been two. There is, first, the important and real question, theologically inspired, whether to number the prefatory statement among the actual commandments or to consider it a highly significant introduction. We believe that the latter view is the more sound, but there is no doubt whatever that the including of the prefatory word as the first of .the commandments gives great force to the theological point: God's mercy precedes his laying down of the covenant requirements; the Decalogue arises in a context of divine grace.

Second, the commandment against the worship of other gods and that against idolatry are brought together by the later additions to the prohibition of idolatry. We shall see below that the

VARIOUS WAYS OF NUMBERING THE TEN COMMANDMENTS[40]

Jewish	Lutheran & Augustine	Roman Catholic	The Commandments in Abbreviated Form (Exod. 20:2–17, RSV)	Reformed Christian	Orthodox Christian	Josephus	Philo
1	—	—	2. I am the Lord your God, who brought you out of the land of Egypt, etc.	—	—	—	—
2	1	1	3. You shall have no other gods before me.	1	1	1	1
2	1	(omitted, or included in 1)	4.–6. You shall not make for yourself a graven image, or any likeness of anything, etc.	2	2	2	2
3	2	2	7. You shall not take the name of the Lord your God in vain, etc.	3	3	3	3
4	3	3	8.–11. Remember the sabbath day, to keep it holy. Six days you shall labor, etc.	4	4	4	4
5	4	4	12. Honor your father and your mother, that your days may be long, etc.	5	5	5	5
6	5	5	13. You shall not kill.	6	6	6	7
7	6	6	14. You shall not commit adultery.	7	7	7	6
8	7	7	15. You shall not steal.	8	8	8	8
9	8	8	16. You shall not bear false witness against your neighbor.	9	9	9	9
10	9 (wife)	9	17 [a]. You shall not covet your neighbor's house;	10	10	10	10
10	10 (rest of Deut. 5:21)	10	[b]. You shall not covet your neighbor's wife, or his manservant, etc.	10	10	10	10
			(Alternative is to use Deut. 5:21, Neither shall you covet your neighbor's wife, etc.)				

reference in 20:5 to "bowing down to *them* and serving *them*" is best taken as referring to the foreign gods, not to the pro hibited idol. But neither of these problems should lead us to the solution of the religious communities listed on the left-hand side of the commandments in the chart on p. 47. The much more plausible enumeration is that found, with very slight variations, by the religious communities listed on the right-hand side of the chart above. Josephus, Philo, and the churches of the Reformed tradition of the Reformation probably have best preserved the enumeration that would have been used in ancient Israel, when the Decalogue was remembered by reference to a particular finger of the right and the left hands.

It is true that with this kind of enumeration we lose any easy scheme for dividing up the "two" tables of the Law into a double collection of five commandments each, or of four and six, which would nicely have fit upon the "original" stone slabs. It may well be, however, that the reference to two tables was intended from the first to refer to two copies of the entire list of the Decalogue, rather than to a division of them. Our own division of the commandments, at any rate, is fourfold. We take the first three commandments to go together as the most fundamental demands of God for the exclusive allegiance of his people. The next two deal with fundamental Israelite institutions, the Sabbath and the family, that can well be grouped together. Next there follow two commandments (killing and adultery) that have in view the most fundamental of protections needed by individual human beings. Finally we have a list of three commandments outlining the most basic of the social obligations required in any society.

I am not sure that the collectors of the commandments, or the initial deliverer of the list to the people, had in mind this distinction within the list. It is nevertheless a very helpful distinction. We now turn to the particular parts of the Decalogue.

PART TWO

EXEGETICAL
STUDIES OF
EACH COMMANDMENT

CHAPTER 3

God's Exclusive Claims

THE "PROLOGUE"

The extravagant claims made for the Ten Commandments seem almost justified when we examine the commandments in detail. At first glance the first three are not revolutionary at all, but when we ponder their meaning for ancient Israel and see what is implied in these prohibitions, we come to see how distinctive they really are.

All three of these first commandments are focused upon the reality of God, of God in relation to the world and to human-kind. With the prefatory words, "I am the Lord your God, who brought you out of the land of Egypt, out of the house of bond-age," all three are tied to the revelation of God to Israel in the time of Moses. They are not, however, presented in such a way as to underline this Israelite connection. They would in all prob-ability have been understood by later Israelites, certainly by the time of the prophet Amos,[1] to be valid for all peoples.

The commandments are addressed to the individual as well as to the community. The second-person singular form of address does not exclude the community as a whole; rather, when we have such a set of requirements introduced as these are intro-duced, it includes the community. Each Israelite is to find the commandments binding, but the commandments fall upon the community of the covenant and thus upon all its members. The familiar shifting of language from "you" to "your forebears" in such confessional passages as Josh. 24:2–13 and Deut. 26:5–11 is not found here in Exodus 20, but the commandments are certainly understood in the same way: God laid these requirements upon the generation present with Moses at the sacred mountain, but the commandments are intended for all Israelites for all time. In fact, as we said, they are presented in such a way as to be felt to be applicable to all individuals and all groups in all times and places.

Such an understanding is implicit in the abrupt way in which Exodus 20 opens: "And God spoke all these words." This speech of God is certainly not clearly prepared for in the closing verses of chap. 19, as we noted above, and it is not explicated in what follows (20:18ff.). Quite deliberately, it seems, the one responsible for placing the Ten Commandments in this location set out to show how unusual and unprecedented the event about to be presented was. We do not learn whether the scene is atop the mountain or in the valley, whether the words are understood to be presented to Moses but in behalf of all the people or whether they are understood to be given to the elders or perhaps to the people as a whole. Striking indeed is this laconic editorial note: "And God spoke all these words."

"I am the Lord your God." Much has been written about whether to translate that way or to translate "I, the Lord, am your God."[2] The difference between the two translations may not be as great as some have made it out to be, but it is still an important difference. In the first translation, emphasis falls upon God's self-identification. God is the one who, according to Exod. 6:2–3, appears under the name "the Lord" or "Yahweh." This very Yahweh who appeared at the sacred mountain to Moses and ordered him to deliver God's people from Egyptian bondage is now appearing to his people to claim their devotion and obedience. God delivered them freely, out of his own love and grace, and in faithfulness to the promise made to the forebears of old. Now God enters into covenant with his people and binds them to himself in allegiance that is unswerving and obedience that is uncompromising.

The other translation, "I, Yahweh, am your God," is not

sharply different from the first, but it takes for granted the name "Yahweh" or "the Lord" for God and puts weight on God's favor extended to this people of his. He is their God, and as their God he wrought deliverance from Egyptian slavery. The same priority of grace is contained in this translation, but less emphasis falls upon the special name of God, a name with its own inner power and meaning, a name which, as heard, should remind the hearers of all that this Yahweh has been and done on behalf of his people.

Given the emphasis upon the meaning and power of God's name, Yahweh (see Exod. 3:14-15, 33:19, and 34:6), the first of these translations seems the more likely. We translate, therefore, "I am the Lord your God who brought you out of the land of Egypt, out of the house of bondage."

The Yahweh who identifies himself to the people is intimately connected with their history and with the history of their deliverance. This prefatory opening, which some interpreters have sought to identify as the "historical prologue" to a treaty, seems to me too short to be the equivalent of such a historical prologue.[3] Instead the phrase stresses God's loving concern for this people upon whom his demands now fall. It is not just that God has a right to place demands upon them, since after all he delivered them from slavery. Rather it is that redemption from bondage is characteristic of Israel's God, just as it is now to be made clear that Israel's God also characteristically places demands upon those with whom he comes into relation. Indeed, it is necessary to underscore the fact that the placing of the covenant demands upon God's people is another, and not by any means the least, of God's gracious historical deeds. God loves Israel so much that he both delivers her from bondage in Egypt and places upon her the requirements of the covenant law.

Is this prologue integral to the list of ten prohibitions? We must answer no. Even if it be the case that from earliest times the list of ten prohibitions was understood to rest upon the grace of the God who had delivered his people from Egyptian slavery, the prologue with God's identification of himself as this redeemer-God would not be one of the commandments in the list or a part of the list as prologue. The prologue, it seems necessary to say, was added.

But when? Probably it was added by Moses at the time of the first oral declaration of the prohibitions and was repeated when the prohibitions were used in the cultic proceedings and presentations of earliest times. There would be real plausibility in our understanding the person making the presentation of the Ten Commandments to the people or to their representatives to preface the reading of them by the words of the prologue: "I am Yahweh your God who brought you out of the land of Egypt, out of the house of bondage." Then follows the set of prohibitions that would also be known by the people from their having learned them in the home and in their own towns and villages and having heard them recited as a summing up of the unqualified and unqualifiable requirements of Yahweh their God. The prologue then belongs to the cultic restatement of the Decalogue, but not to its bare listing as a set of prohibitions capable of enumeration on the ten fingers.

THE FIRST COMMANDMENT: NO OTHER GODS
"THOU SHALT NOT HAVE OTHER GODS"

This first commandment should be seen in relation to others that are closely akin to it. Among the oldest such commandments in the Hebrew Scriptures is Exod. 22:20: "Whoever sacrifices to any god, except to the Lord alone, shall be put to the ban" (Hebrew, 22:19). The commandment that opens the Decalogue certainly does not presuppose a monotheistic position on the part of the author. Rather, it presupposes the existence, at least the theoretical existence, of other gods. At the same time, the commandment makes it clear that the community of Israel is not to credit such gods with any significance or power over their lives.

Our discussion of this commandment, and of all ten commandments, must take into account the contents of the received text and not deal only with our reconstructed text. In the case of the first commandment, the two are almost identical. We have only the expression "before me" (Hebrew: 'al panay) to add in order to have the commandment handed down by tradition. How is this expression to be understood? We probably can get as near to the center of meaning of this commandment without it as we can with it. Taken literally, the commandment may mean that no other gods are to appear at the cultic sites where Yahweh is worshiped. That would in effect mean that the first commandment is prohibiting the making of images of gods other than Yahweh or of showing veneration to such gods at the places where Yahweh is worshiped. It may well be that at some quite early stage of Israelite religion there developed such a commandment. Exodus 22:20 (Hebrew, 22:19) would seem to indicate that this was in fact the case. See also Deut. 27:15, a prohibition of the making of images, which could mean images of any kind of God but especially images of other gods.

Much more likely is the meaning that Israel is prohibited from taking as rivals to Yahweh any of the gods of the ancient Near Eastern world. Yahweh is a jealous God, tolerating no rivals, as the addition to the second commandment makes clear (Exod. 20:5-6). None of the gods of the ancient world, then, is to be a rival to Yahweh. They do not come before Yahweh, nor do they come before the worshipers of Yahweh. They exist, of course, and have their adherents in the world, but among the people of Israel such gods must be understood not to count.

Thus far our first commandment pins down several absolutely basic realities for early Israelite religion. The God who appears with his demands is Yahweh. He identifies himself by that name and also by reference to the deeds of salvation that brought the people here to the mountain. There are other gods in the world of ancient Israel, but none of them counts, or is permitted to count, for Israel.

This was, in its day, a remarkable position for the early Israelites to have reached in their religious pilgrimage. Only a few generations earlier, in the time of the patriarchs Abraham and Isaac and Jacob, the Israelites or their ancestors were developing a religious position in which the God of the forefather was understood as chief God, one related to the tribe or clan as head of the family, and who accompanied the tribe in its movements from the settled land of Canaan to the pastoral lands of the east and south, and back again, as the people followed their double vocation of pastoral and agricultural existence. Now, surely to some degree as a result of the work of the man Moses, Israel is commanded to take account of no god other than Yahweh, the one who brought them from bondage to freedom and who now, identifiable by his name Yahweh, demands their full allegiance.

When we look at this first commandment, however, we can take note of the important development in ancient Israel's religious understanding but still ask ourselves whether the commandment has any continuing force for us. It is not entirely defensible, in all likelihood, to substitute for "gods" the items of our contemporary life that preoccupy us and divert us from concern for God and fellow human beings, items such as money, position, and security. Does the commandment have any really significant word for contemporary human beings?

Certainly the question foremost in our minds as we hear this commandment is not the existence of gods other than Yahweh, the true God of Jewish or Christian faith. Rather, we might well consider, if challenged, whether we believe in the existence of God at all. We may well want to reply in the affirmative, since it would perhaps seem to us rash to deny the existence of God. Even so, the idea that our lives are claimed by a God who is our deliverer and redeemer, who will brook no rivals but demands our fullest allegiance, and who ringingly declares that we are to have no gods before him—such an idea can hardly be entertained seriously by the secularized citizens of the Western world.

Or so we may well suppose. Who can be sure, however, of such a statement? Is it not the case that many, many persons in this secularized and de-divinized world long for nothing else so much as for God, for the living God, hungering and thirsting for that which can be understood to be the very ground and center of their de-divinized lives? We cannot satisfy such a longing by the hypothetical reimposition of the existence of the God of Israel into our lives. We may well find, however, that our own lives, like our own tradition as a people, bear testimony in a variety of ways to the same reality identified by ancient Israel as

"Yahweh who brought them out of the land of Egypt, out of the house of bondage."

The testimony of many, at any rate, is that their personal existence shows such a dimension of mysterious meaning coming to the surface that they cannot give account of personal existence from the this-worldly side of existence alone. There are such dimensions of personal cruelty to others, uncalled for and inexplicable, just as there are such dimensions of personal caring and love for others, again uncalled for and inexplicable, that one has to advert to the essential Mystery of being.[4]

Given this dimension of existence that is confirmed in our own personal existence, we are able to compare the claim of this Mystery being disclosed to the claim of the God of ancient Israel who will brook no rivals at all. The comparison is not too close, not until there are identifying marks to the Mystery. The imposition of the identifying marks of ancient Israel involves a step that is for many a giant one. I was not in Egypt, God has not brought me from slavery to freedom, and there are no rival powers in my life that vie for absolute allegiance. There is at most a recognition of a deep hunger for abiding meaning in life, plus some signs that such meaning does find expression in my life. I may, however, be unable to make a pattern of such emergences of meaning and relate the pattern to the story of biblical redemption.

Yet we should not be too quick to deny the claim of this first commandment upon us. To have no *other* gods is to be possessed by the one God. And we are, many of us, aware of a fundamental reality, deeper than any surface analysis of our contemporary history, claiming our lives and placing upon us the inescapable bond of allegiance to this reality, first and last. Nothing in all our experience can be compared with this deepest and most all-encompassing reality. There is a presence, a Thou, a One, disclosed to us in faith and unmistakably testified to in the course of our own existence as individuals and as members of groups. To the extent that such a presence is known by us who live in the secularized Western world, to that extent the commandment is by no means without its significance or power.

The power that it exercises, under those conditions, however, is felt to be not so much a matter of coercive demand as of declaration. God, the One who enters our lives and discloses elements of our history as individuals and as members of the particular human community to which we belong, claims our lives as just this one who is incomparable, as power and presence unprecedented, as at once fearsome and loving, causing us to draw back in holy dread lest we be destroyed, and also impelling us forward into yet closer association and communion.

The commandments remain commandments, but they take on a character different from ordinary prohibitions or demands, as we shall see more fully as our study of the Decalogue proceeds. It is the self-evidently right thing to do not to have any gods before us other than the Lord alone. What possible sense could it make to give allegiance to other gods when the very terms of revelation of this God make it foolish to give halfhearted allegiance or partial allegiance? Even so, the commandment does not take on the form of later prophetic pronouncements about Yahweh's incomparability or about the folly of idolatry, such as we find in Isaiah 40–55 (see 40:18–20, 25–26; 44:6–8; 45: 5–7).[5] It is not a summons to monotheism but a call to recognize that only the Lord counts for those who know the story of the Lord's acts of salvation and deliverance or who have an equivalent in their own lives.

And what of those who do not know the story of God's deliverance? Can this commandment come to life and take on meaning for them? From what was said above, there is every reason to suppose that deep within each human being is such a story of salvation, such a dimension of meeting with the Holy One, the authentic and true Presence. The story of God's salvation of Israel or the Christian church has a richness and depth and amplitude about it that may well entitle us to claim much for this story. We need not, however, suppose that it is without counterpart in the life of other peoples or in the depths of the self of any or every human being.

What, then, is a violation of this first of the commandments? We have argued against any spiritualizing or allegorizing of the commandment. Those who put their trust in wealth or position or social acceptance and seek these in such a way as to give them ultimate significance are making gods of them, it is often said, and we can recognize the truth in such an observation without accepting it as an adequate truth. No, the placing of other gods before Yahweh, according to biblical religion, is an act of double-mindedness. One first gives full allegiance to the God of Israel, the Holy One, and then withdraws the fullness of that allegiance and "limps between two opinions" (a probable translation of the difficult Hebrew text in 1 Kings 18:21, where Elijah addresses the Israelite community and demands that they place their full trust in Yahweh).

Would ancient Israel also have found it equally a violation of the divine commandment to have denied the existence of God? Apparently not. In biblical times, an atheist was a fool (Ps. 14:1 and 53:1), misguided, or silly, but not necessarily evil-minded. In our own time, too, I think it evident that many agnostics and atheists are quite simply unable to give much weight to the dimensions of essential Mystery that we spoke of above. It is no violation of the first commandment to ask, "But is there such a reality as is here spoken of, that which or the One who claims our fullest and undivided allegiance?" Certainly, there is no way to demonstrate by analyses of contemporary historical existence or to convince by logical analysis that such a central reality exists. Nor is there a way by the use of such forms of examination to demonstrate that such a reality lacks existence.[6]

We remain, then, with a commandment prefaced by a claim of faith and always presupposing a kind of prior faith. Is there a way to rewrite the first commandment to make it more telling and plausible as a prohibition for any human being today who honors the fundamental Mystery of being? We might suggest such a reformulation as "Thou shalt not deny that Being is One." We might prefer "Thou shalt not take account of more than one fundamental reality in life." Only God is God, and God— creator, sustainer, and consummator of all that has being—tolerates no rivals.

As we look backward at the discussion of this first commandment we may be able to feel its weight and power more directly.

There is One who claims human beings, each human being and in particular the human beings for whom the biblical disclosures have come to be the very story of their lives. This One who claims us insists upon being the One who alone may claim our lives absolutely. There are to be no rivals, there is to be no divided reality, there are no longer to be mysteries manifold. There is only one essential Mystery: a mysterious power and presence coming to disclosure, unbidden by human beings, often, but coming whether invited or no. To set other powers that are manifest in the world alongside this One, sensible as that may appear, is not permitted. Why? Because it is a denial of the very reality that most grounds the hunger for fundamental meaning and unity in life; it would undercut the hunger that impels human beings on the religious quest, a hunger that finds satisfaction in the oneness of God. It is not a mere monism, for the one who places the demand is Yahweh the deliverer from bondage, the one who marks oppression and will not forever endure it, the one who sends human agents to do battle against the powers of oppression and darkness.

And here is where the hunger for unity is most significant and where the significance of the first commandment may lie. We will not find the meaning or the sense of purpose that we seek apart from the recognition of this incomparable unity of being and meaning in the one God. We can see in the history of religions how dangerous the bifurcation of the religious substance in fact is. While it is much more "sensible" to see the world as divided into the powers that do damage and the powers that promote the good, such a view of the world ends in an irreconcilable hunger for the one Mystery. And all sorts of perils for human life on earth lurk in such a religious position. When dualism is fundamental, the world of God's creation is devalued, and with it human life. When God is not also to some degree recognized as the "source" of the evils that befall humankind, either the religion ends as trivial and not really significant for human life at all—a thin religious humanism with no challenge to the evil that human beings do to one another—or God is not really struggled with for blessing in the way that the biblical psalmists did.[7]

The first commandment, then, is the commandment that takes the reality of God seriously: as creator of the universe, as the sustainer of all beings and all being, and as the one whose purposes move forward to their consummation. To commit oneself to have no other gods is to commit oneself to the one holy Mystery, the truth that all life is dependent at every moment upon the One who grounds all that has being. Small wonder that many have found in the first commandment the summary import of the entire Ten Commandments, or the foundation of biblical religion as a whole.

I suspect that the addition "before my face" was a quite early addition. It underscored, when it was made, what has been said above. God is not denying, according to this religious disclosure, that there are other powers in the world that claim the allegiance of human beings and do so at a very deep level. But none of the powers and mysteries of the realm of human experience is to be understood to stand on God's level at all. God is, as Second Isaiah is to point out in lyrical language, incomparable, beyond likeness in anything that is to be found in all the world. And unity for the life of human beings is found here, in the radical monotheism of biblical religion. Christians should be grateful that their forebears insisted upon this point in the controversies of the early Christian centuries. The doctrine of the Holy Trinity is a way of affirming precisely the unity of God and God's unique relation to everything and every being in the whole of creation.

THE SECOND COMMANDMENT: NO IMAGE OF GOD "THOU SHALT NOT MAKE FOR THYSELF AN IDOL"

If the first commandment is the comprehensive one, the touchstone for all biblical religion, the second commandment is clearly the most striking and distinctive, with the possible exception of the fourth (the Sabbath commandment). Here too we may suppose at first glance that the commandment is not at all revolutionary, given what we know about biblical religion and about the course of religious development in the ancient Near Eastern world. If we simply took for granted the progress in religion from lower understandings to higher ones that we often assume must have occurred, with the help of the Hebrew poets and prophets, then the shedding of superstition and of the need for material representations of God would seem to follow from such religious development and progress.

Actually, the higher religions (higher by most standards) are the ones that know how to provide a place for representations of the deity in material form. Far from being a mark of crude religious understanding, the making of representatives of the divine powers is a highly sophisticated religious practice and rests upon a well-developed understanding of how the transcendent world is to find its depiction here on the material earth.[8] The Israelite break with the making of images is an extraordinarily radical break with the high and profound religious understandings of the world of Israel's neighbors. Even so, the prohibition has a profundity of its own that is all the more striking, given the reasons for the representation of the deity in images that have been alive in the world for so long.

Indeed, the development of an understanding of the overarching heavens as the realm of the gods and of fundamental, "archetypal" reality, of which the earthly realm is a representation or manifestation or copy, lies behind the making of representatives of the gods as it lies behind much of the religious practice and understanding of humankind. It is the central religious conception of the peoples of the ancient Near East and continues to be of enormous influence in religious practices and understandings throughout the entire world today. Plato's philosophy depends upon this fundamental distinction between the heavenly world of the archetypes and the manifest world of nature and history. It is a conception on which the biblical writers also depended, although they were the first of the ancient peoples radically to modify this conception.[9] This radical modification is summed up in its briefest possible form in the original prohibition: "Thou shalt not make for thyself an idol."

The commandment insists that there is in fact no reality on earth that suffices to provide the representation of the deity. But surely the people of biblical times would have known that such a representative was that and not more, that the image of God was not identical with the high God of the heavenly reaches, the great Lord Marduk or Baal or Asshur. Why not have such a focus on earth of the high God? Surely religious faith would only be strengthened by such a representation. As we know from the several stories of creation, ancient Near Eastern folk believed in the power of the high God as a creator of the earth and its goods. Ancient Israel also knew the God of the forebears, knew Yahweh who led the Israelites from Egypt, as the Creator of heaven and earth. Stories of creation in the surrounding cultures did not lead those who used and depended upon these stories to make the distinction that Israel apparently made between the Creator and all created things. How is such a commandment to be understood? What lies behind it? Is there any way to trace the development of the notion that is at the heart of the second commandment?

Gerhard von Rad has made popular the idea that the Israelites were unwilling to accept the notion that God's own future for his people Israel could in any sense be represented in an image.[10] Rather, that ambiguous and open-ended future of God with Israel meant that the people had to get their signs as to God's character and purpose from the history they shared with God, a history full of ambiguity and at the same time pointing to God's faithfulness to the promise made to the forefathers.

The contrast between a static image and the dynamic movement of historical existence is an important one and may well contribute to the development of this commandment. There is more at stake, however. What the person or persons initially responsible for this commandment thought about Yahweh is the decisive point. Why should Yahweh reject any image of himself, no matter what it resembled—bird, animal, fish, or human being? Why this iconoclasm? Yahweh is certainly portrayed in language and story as actively involved in the life of his people— walking with them, showing anger at their sins, coming to their aid in time of danger, and comforting, admonishing, and threatening them. Why should Yahweh not be ready to have himself represented in plastic imagery as he certainly is represented, with no great reservations by most of Israelite tradition, in language?

I have come to believe that Moses' own discovery that Yahweh is the incomparable one, the unrepresentable one, is at the heart of the prohibition. No material of the created world suffices to represent Yahweh, because the distinction between Creator and creature is already, in Moses' own lifetime, felt to be so vast. The actual theological working out of the distinction between the Creator and the created world and all creatures will come later; but in Moses' own life the necessity to insist on this distinction came.

The priestly tradition later explicates, in its own way, what lies behind the prohibition. God makes human beings in his own image and likeness and thus sees them as closest of all the creatures of earth to God the Creator. Making images of God in any form is providing a representation of God that will not suffice and cannot be permitted. It stands in the way of seeing God as the living God, the best possible representation of whom is the human being, the living human being bearing God's breath of life. No cultic representation can do justice to the living God; only human beings can be a kind of representation of God on earth, and they must be such a representation not at the cult center where their representation is set up, but in daily life, demonstrating faithfulness to the commandments of the God who created them.

In these first two commandments, then, we have a double insistence upon the exclusive claim of Yahweh upon his people. The first commandment makes clear that God will brook no rival at all. The second indicates that human beings cannot find in the world of God's creation any adequate representation of Yahweh. They cannot suppose that any of the created things in God's world can be shaped to provide an adequate representation of Yahweh. There is only one kind of representation that God will endure: the representation provided by a faithful human community bent on doing God's will on earth.

Such an understanding of the second commandment does not fully account for what is found in the present, expanded text of the commandment. The explication of a likeness (temunah) of anything in the entire creation is still on the mark and fits the interpretation given above. The reference to bowing down and

serving *them* is clearly a reference to images of other gods, forbidden by the first commandment. The picture of Yahweh as a
jealous God, visiting the iniquities of the fathers upon the children up to the third or the fourth generation, also fits the first
commandment more directly than it fits the second. Even so, it
is appropriate to the second, since God will not have human
beings misunderstand their own relation to him and seek to make
plastic representations of the deity.

And there are two sides to these commandments, as John
Calvin showed so clearly in his exposition of them in the *Institutes.*[11] Israel is to make no image of Yahweh, but Israel is to
be such an image of God in the world. God is jealous of his
prerogatives, but God is delighted to shower mercy upon those
who love him and keep his commandments. When the people of
Israel are faithful to the God of the covenant, then God has the
right kind of representative in the world of humankind.

Viewed in such a light, the second commandment unmistakably shows its import in today's world. The understandable
disposition of a religious community is to find bearable ways in
which to represent the claims and the power of God. One such
way is the provision of cultic worship itself, the identification of
the sacred times and places where the Holy prefers to disclose
itself; the selection of persons skilled in the mediation between
the Holy One and the community; the fixing of certain modes of
cultic activity that at once bring the sacred power near and
diminish the likelihood of the power's doing us harm rather than
good. Cult and worship thus run the very grave danger of neu-
tralizing the claims of God upon the very people who in the cult
seek to bring those claims into effective force.

When a representative of the deity is added, then the temptation is made the greater that the representation will all the more
effectively assist the community to neutralize the explosive power
present at the appearing of the Holy. The Israelites certainly
sought to neutralize the dangerous power of the Holy in all kinds
of ways, ways quite in keeping with those used by other ancient
Near Eastern peoples. They had their cultic rites, they observed
their sacred seasons at the appointed cultic sites, and they ap-

pointed a class of Israelites to see to the trafficking with the Holy that was essential to their life. They had an ark of the covenant that, at various times, would have been understood as a representation of Yahweh in very much the same way that images of Yahweh would have been understood. They had cherubim standing alongside the ark as the latter (in whatever form at that time) was placed within the Holy of Holies of the temple built by Solomon. They had the golden calf of the wilderness period (Exodus 32) and the golden calves or bulls of Bethel and Dan (1 Kings 12).[12]

But such representations were not permitted to be understood by Israel's theologians as images of Yahweh. No legitimate image of Yahweh was possible. No created thing could provide such a representation; moreover, Israel, God's people, was to represent God's cause in the world. It is the vocation of Israel as the people of God that stands athwart the path leading to the making of representations of Yahweh. No idolatry is permitted, because God will have a people in the world that is God's firstborn son, appointed to serve God and to represent God's cause in the world (Exod. 4:22–23).[13]

Limits, then, are imposed upon Israel's worship from the very outset, in all likelihood by Moses himself. God is certainly to be worshiped, and there is no reason to suppose that early Israel was at all puritanical or iconoclastic in its worship of Yahweh. But one limit is deep and pervasive: do not set up any representative of Yahweh at your cultic sites, and do not keep such a representative in your villages or settlements or in your own tents or homes. Who represents Yahweh in the world and among the nations? Yahweh's people and no other reality. The human being, male and female, is made in God's image and likeness, and no other creature is so made. Living human beings cannot be set up on pedestals at cultic sites, but living human beings doing God's will and work in the world are testimonies to the active presence and power of God in the world.

Put in the context of our contemporary world, such a view of the meaning of the second commandment shows us its power and import. People today in our circles may not be tempted to make representations of the deity of wood or stone or metal or any other substance, but people of our own generation are certainly tempted to fail to be adequate representatives of God on earth in the fullness of their own humanity.

It is also the case that throughout the generations human beings have been all too ready to represent the divine power imperfectly, in created objects or in institutions that serve as representatives of God on earth. We reminded ourselves not to spiritualize the first commandment by suggesting that the worship of money or position or security was the equivalent of worshiping other gods. Now we need also to say that the setting up of such material realities as representatives of God is probably not the same thing as the making of images of God, but it is a closer thing. The representation of the "divine" power in sex or in glossolalia or in some absolutely authoritative biblical interpretation would seem to be a representation of God through creaturely beings in violation of the second commandment.

The second commandment is more violated by what we fail to do than by what we do. We fail to claim our place as human beings, charged to be a representation of the cause and the claim of God on earth, identifiable as God's firstborn child, ready to serve God, committed to let the peoples of earth know what it means to live consciously as those created in God's image and likeness. Our temptation is not to identify the creature with the Creator, to claim a kind of power for our representation of God on earth that should not be claimed for any created thing. Our greater temptation is to miss the corollary of the second commandment: that God will have only one kind of representation on earth, one that is close to his very nature and power—human beings made in his image, and a community called out to embody this vocation before the nations of earth. Every human being is made in God's image and likeness. No image of God can be made for ourselves. Those are the two realities that need to be held together today. When they are, we see what moral force this second commandment actually has.

We should note, however, that human beings represent God's cause in the world not primarily in spiritual ways but in very concrete and practical ones. They represent God's concern for a clean and beautiful earth, a productive earth, one filled with the full variety of the creatures called into being at the Creation. They represent God's concern for the sharing of the goods of earth in a tolerably fair way, for the maintenance of life and its possibilities, for the furthering of the institutional arrangements that preserve life and make it flower. The second commandment thus introduces us in advance to the intentions and qualities of the commandments to follow.

But we must ask whether the Israelites did not pay too dear a price for this refusal to make representations of God. There can be no doubt that the making of images of the gods gave to ancient communities a sense of the closeness of the heavens and enabled them to participate in the power of the transcendent realm with great effectiveness and continuity. How did the early Israelites find a comparable way of participating in the reality of the transcendent world?

The answer is partly given in the community's concentration upon the earthly realities themselves. The break with a notion of archetypal reality in the heavens in favor of an archetypal period in the early history of humankind (reflected in the stories of the Creation, the Flood, the times of the patriarchs) and of Israel (Exodus, wanderings, entrance into the land of Canaan) was a radical one and clearly finds reflection in our second commandment. But were these earthly archetypes capable of bearing the weight laid upon them?

What was this weight? When we look at the religions of the Mesopotamian, Canaanite, and Egyptian worlds and consider the place of the images of their deities, we might better discern the commandment's significance. Throughout these cultures we can see how much the best art of the peoples was lavished upon the production of objects of worship, and especially upon the framing of representatives of the transcendent world. This artistic work and the care of the craftspeople were accompanied by great sacrifices of time, energy, and material wealth. The best was set apart to be given to the worship of the high gods and to the representation of them upon earth. Around the temples and the cult objects in the temples were focused many of the skills of their civilization: writing, developed largely to pass along the stories of the beginnings of things, including the origin of the transcendent world's creatures and of their calling the earthly world into existence; the arts of construction; ways of preserving the dead or of providing suitable and therefore beautiful places for their bodies to rest; hymns and laments with which to evoke the high gods to come to the aid of the community; wisdom traditions with which to help hold the society together by means of information passed along from the transcendent realm.

Without the prohibition of the making of images, it seems highly probable that Israelite religion would have fitted much more comfortably into the pattern of ancient Near Eastern religion. The Israelites were moved in the direction of such a pattern over and over again; the making of young bulls for the sanctuaries at Bethel and Dan was such a move. Worship upon the hills at the "high places" throughout much of Israel's history certainly involved a move in the direction of representations of the high gods through standing stones and occasionally through forbidden representation of the female and male deities of the West Semitic cultures. The theologians were ready, however, to challenge and to assault such practices as they emerged, however innocent or indeed religiously useful they may have been.

In place of this kind of commitment to the lavishing upon the high gods of one's best aesthetic gifts and one's most precious material possessions, the Israelites made their contributions. They developed literature concretely tied to their historical and cultural existence. They saw Yahweh as related to daily life in ways different from the relation of the other high gods to the daily life of their societies. God, they came to believe, was shaping a people in the world through whom blessing must go forth to all the peoples of the earth. God demanded commitment to the needs of human beings, the practice of responsible social and cultural relations that took into account the needs of people other than simply the ones in charge of things.

These Israelites also devoted much of their attention to the same religious concerns that absorbed their neighbors' attention:

how to secure the favor of God here on earth. With no representations of the deities in their temples, the Israelites had to bring
the reality of Yahweh before the people in song and hymn and
lament. The theophany hymn takes on very special importance
by the time of the establishment of the temple in Jerusalem.
Cultic singers would describe the coming of Yahweh to the holy
place, his sweeping in upon the wings of the wind, passing over
the gathered crowd, invisibly taking his stand atop the ark of
the covenant as it made its way into the Holy of Holies through
solemn procession. There Yahweh was, not visible to the eye, of
course, but there unmistakably. This dynamic story of the coming of Yahweh to the cult center gave to the people of Israel the
same sense of the actual presence of God at the cult site that
the ancient Canaanite had of Baal's presence in his temple. But a
great responsibility fell upon the poets who composed these
poems: enabling the assembled worshipers to sense and feel and
detect that presence of the Holy that in other societies would
have been much more easily and vividly portrayed through the
images of the deity.

The same responsibility fell upon prophet and priest and wise
person: to provide a people having an imageless cult and imageless society those concrete representations of the deity that
otherwise came through the images. And therein we can see how
the second commandment served the community so well. It drove
the Israelites to find ways to portray the presence of Yahweh in
their daily life: in the affairs of government, in warfare, in the
rendering of judgment, in teaching the young, in the whole net-
work of social relations among neighbors, and in the treatment of
strangers. The need to represent Yahweh's presence in these
other ways, without the aid of the plastic image, probably did
much to intensify the Israelites' search for the signs of God's presence in these affairs of daily life.

But how could the community have come to such a view?
What origin can we give for this commandment? Does it come
before the first commandment and lead to the framing of the
first? It does indeed appear to be older than the first command-

ment and to prompt the creation of the first. I believe that we are on safe ground in assigning to the man Moses the discovery that Yahweh will not permit the framing of any image of himself. Moses' double relation with the rich polytheism of Egypt and its representation of the deities in many forms there and with the Midianites (perhaps the Kenites within the larger entity called Midianites) provided cultural impetus to this discovery. But the fact is that nothing quite explains or accounts for such a step in the history of religious understanding and practice, just as nothing will quite account for the appearance of the observance of a seventh day of rest. Moses apparently was convinced that the God who had appeared to him would tolerate no representation of himself because any such representation would do violence to the very nature of the God Yahweh. This Yahweh was explosive power, bent upon active leadership of his people in this world and intent upon the people's recognition of his demand that their daily life be in conformity with his own will and desires. Moses quickly learns of this fierce exclusiveness of Yahweh, the God who appeared to him, and Moses slowly works out its terms and begins the process of developing ways to account for that exclusiveness and to explain it.

The first commandment follows upon the second. The same God who will tolerate no representation of himself is the one who will not permit rival powers around him. The elaboration of the second commandment, then, to insist that nothing in all the world of God's creation can serve to represent God, and further that no one is to bow down to or serve such representations of Yahweh, makes it evident that the two commandments are being interpreted together by the later tradition. Yahweh is a jealous God who will not tolerate rivals, and that jealousy is really what is behind the insistence that no image be made of him. Yahweh cannot be controlled or manipulated. The existence of the plastic representation invites the community to believe otherwise, even when the theology of representation of the deity through plastic images does not rest upon such an understanding.

And thus we are prepared for our examination of the third

commandment, the import of which is to rule out the ways human beings seek to control the power of the Holy and direct it toward their own desired ends.

THE THIRD COMMANDMENT:
NO MISUSE OF GOD'S POWER
"THOU SHALT NOT LIFT UP THE NAME OF YAHWEH FOR MISCHIEF"

The third commandment, as noted above, carries out the theme of Yahweh's exclusive claims upon his people. Yahweh's power is available for the maintenance of the world and for the care and protection (as well as the discipline) of his people. The tradition keeps alive the sense of God's presence and guidance in history, and the cult makes vivid that presence and enables worshipers to claim that power. But there is a limit beyond which the community and its individual members dare not go in the claiming and use of God's power. That limit is the subject of the third commandment.

The translation is not without its complexities and difficulties. We might well ask whether the passage should not read "Thou shalt not lift up my name for mischief." Why should we not translate, when we are trying to reconstruct the original form of the commandment, with the use of the first-person singular pronoun? The commandments are certainly set forth as direct prohibitions, addressed (in the second-person singular) to the community and its members. Is not God the speaker? He is so identified in the prologue of v. 2. In the cultic use of the Ten Commandments there is no doubt that Yahweh himself will have been understood to be the speaker.

Even so, we believe that it is better to keep in view the larger cultural and traditional contexts within which the Ten Commandments came to claim the life of ancient Israel and were preserved. That includes the cult, but it also includes the family and the clan, the village and town. The recollection of the Ten Commandments by reference to the ten fingers is itself a clear indication of how pervasive the presence of these prohibitions must have been in ancient Israelite society. Thus it is wise to retain the translation that leaves the name "Yahweh" in the commandment. It may be that we should translate without the use of the "of"; in that way, the emphasis would fall upon the prohibition of misuse of the name "Yahweh" and would leave ambiguous whether someone was referring to Yahweh in the third person. We know from the psalms and the prophetic literature that Yahweh can speak through some human voice in the first person and then occasionally refer to himself in the third person. Not too much, therefore, should be drawn from this reference to Yahweh by name, so far as the original setting of the commandments is concerned. Eduard Nielsen is quite content with the reference in the third person, because he is of the view that the commandments are from a ninth-century North Israelite king and constitute the proclamation of a collection of prohibitions as a kind of royal legal edict.[14] I am convinced that Nielsen's picture of the origin of the collection is unsatisfactory. The crediting of the emergence of the Decalogue to such a period in Israelite history and under the circumstances that he reconstructs is much less plausible than the assigning of the collection as a whole to the general period of Moses, where both the social/cultural and the cultic contexts would be entirely suited to the appearance of the collection.

The translation "for mischief" also calls for comment. The Hebrew expression *laššāw'* has often been translated "in vain," with the meaning to treat Yahweh's name lightly, to use it idly, to treat it with light contempt. I do not find any occurrences clearly supporting such a translation. The word is stronger than such a translation indicates. It is used in parallelism, or near parallelism, with *tō 'ēvāh* in Isa. 1:13: "Bring no more vain offerings; incense is an abomination to me." A much better translation would be "Bring no more destructive offerings" or "offensive offerings." Rather than being an expression for emptiness or insubstantiality, the term carries with it active power for harm.

Using Yahweh's name for mischief means misusing the power inherent in the personal name for God to do harm against others. The magical or almost magical power inherent in a name is reflected in this commandment. The prohibition is against the use of Yahweh's name to invoke curses upon another person or to conjure up evil spirits by the use of the power-laden name or otherwise to take advantage of one's knowledge of the powerful personal name of the deity. Ancient Israelites were reluctant to use God's personal name in their pronouncement of curses. I suspect it was early in Israelite life that the prohibition against such misuse of the divine name developed, and probably once again it was Moses who was responsible for the formulation we have.

The use of God's personal name in oath-taking was quite all right as long as it was done with care and as long as one was not swearing falsely (see the ninth commandment). Calling for blessing from God to come to anyone was also quite all right. It was the dark side to the reality of God that was not to be used by the adherents of Yahwism to do mischief against the fellow human beings. This dark side of religion is widely recognized today as present in virtually all dynamic religious experience. It is unmistakably present in ancient Israel. Religion arises in considerable part as a means for the prevention of harm from the high god rather than as a means of securing blessing. The destructive forces are everywhere in evidence to ancient folk, and means must be found to avert the harm that they threaten to loose upon human beings and upon the world.

As one learns how to avert harm, one naturally and apparently inevitably learns how to inflict harm. For this reason, a commandment like the third is central to such a list as the Decalogue. It is very difficult to be sure that more good has been done by religion than harm; human beings have such capacity to twist and distort the good things of life and make them instruments of damage to fellow human beings and to the world that one might almost despair at such perverse misuse of the goods and disclosures of religion.[15] So it is with the name of God. Not to know the name is not to be in touch with the depth of the power being made accessible to worshipers through the revelation of the high god. If the name of the deity is withheld, much that might otherwise be available to the worshiping community is not yet available. We see this hungering on the part of Moses for the name of God in several places, and in each of them the name is given, but not fully given.[16] It was apparently Moses himself who was responsible for this disclosure to his followers that the God revealed on the sacred mountain gave the name "Yahweh" to Moses to pronounce. But with the name, Moses did not receive the hidden, inner meaning of the name. In some such way we have to understand the awkward Hebrew sentence *'eheyeh 'asher 'eheyeh* in Exod. 3:14. I translate the sentence "I am who I am (and I will say no more)." Note that in Exod. 33:19, where Moses wishes to see God's glory, Moses is told that God "will be gracious to whom [he] will be gracious and will show mercy on whom [he] will show mercy." God refuses to let the fullness of his name's meaning be known.

Yet the name Yahweh is clearly full of power, and its misuse must be protected against. Hence the commandment. Israel must not make religion into a club or weapon with which to have its way over others. Religion must not be a tool for frightening persons and groups to do the bidding of the religious authorities. It must not be an instrument for the benefit of those who know the religious secrets. But who can deny that religion often is precisely that? Hosea spoke about the priests who "feed upon the sins of the people" and are "greedy for their iniquity" (4:8). Amaziah charges Amos with being a prophet who threatens doom against North Israel in order to make a living and feed his belly (Amos 7:12). In our own day we know well enough how those charged with providing religious leadership often find ways to twist the words of judgment into instruments of fear and intimidation, maintaining their financial empires by threats against sinners in the name of God. The use of the divine name for mischief is not restricted to threats of hellfire; equally appalling, I believe, is the issuing of palliatives in the name of religion, offering soothing syrup in place of a demand for justice, or speaking "peace, peace when there is no peace," or "healing the sins of a people lightly." That is what Hosea probably saw in North Israel when he spoke of "feeding on the sins of the people."

Another way in which the word of power is misused for mischief is in the concentration upon joy and delight in the Lord and in life that has no roots or substance, upon the proclaiming of a love and forgiveness of God that knows no demands but only invites that most tricky of all religious summonses: to share life in the Spirit with "us." Authentic movements of the Spirit know the stern demands of the God of justice and know that the path of faith is one that takes its toll upon those who walk in it. Superficial invitations to "conversion" or to "renewal in the Spirit" are in their way just as dangerous as threats of eternal punishment upon the sinners whom we wish to convert to our particular brand of religious faith. And all are equally misuses of the power in the name of God.

We can see, therefore, that this third commandment has a burning import for our common life today, and in particular for organized religion. We can see, too, why in early times the community added to the commandment this clause: "for Yahweh will not hold the one guiltless who lifts up his name for mischief." God will not endure such a misuse of power designed to bring health and healing. When religion is turned perversely against the very means that it uses to bring blessing, then the springs are poisoned and little can be done. How massive is the damage that has been done by those who have lifted up God's name for mischief. Thousands and thousands struggle for health in mental institutions trying to undo, with professional help, the damage done by those who have driven them into psychosis by the warnings of eternal damnation. Unloved in this world by family and friends, as they believe, they have concluded that God too will not love them, cannot love them, until they do what the religious practitioner demands they do. God, too, may then be identified as a deceiver and destroyer. These more subtle ways of abusing the power of God are far more destructive, I believe, than those prevalent in ancient societies.

The first three commandments focus together upon Yahweh's exclusive claim upon the people for whom these commandments were binding. All have in view the preface telling of Yahweh's gracious act of deliverance from Egyptian slavery. All presuppose the love and grace of the God who places these demands upon them. And all drive home with vigor the fundamental necessity for God's people to observe these prohibitions. No penalties are stated. There is a lean, clean brevity of speech. God simply lays down the basic kinds of human activity that are not permissible, not tolerable, not by any means to be done. To add threats would be unnecessary and would weaken the force of such a lean and astringent set of prohibitions. Where in all the Hebrew Scriptures do we get a clearer picture not simply of what the God of Israel will not tolerate from his creatures but also of the very character of this God? God, the deliverer from Egyptian bondage, will not have people lavish upon him their gifts of gold and silver and jewelry and other bounties in an effort to placate him, or buy him off from demanding righteousness of them. God will not let them use the unmistakable power that they have through knowing his name to do harm to their enemies. God remains the determiner of how the power inherent in his name is to be used. And God will not permit them to make images of him from any goods of earth, for nothing in all the earth can adequately show his true nature and character. Human beings are to live and act in such a way as to enable other human beings to know more and more about the nature and character of God. If people want to know more about the God of Israel, they should be able to look to the people redeemed from bondage in Egypt and find out about that God.

CHAPTER 4

God's Basic Institutions

THE FOURTH COMMANDMENT:
NO WORK ON THE SEVENTH DAY
"THOU SHALT NOT DESPISE THE SABBATH DAY"

The prohibition of work on the seventh day of the week by ancient Israel is a unique custom in the ancient Near Eastern world. It is true that there were days of ill omen in ancient Babylonia on which it was inauspicious to do certain things or to commence various undertakings. It is also true that in the ancient world there were market days, days set aside for the exchanges of goods in various localities, with the consequent suspension of ordinary labor while goods were bartered and exchanged. And there were special days set aside for cultic worship in connection with the phases of the moon, with the new moon and full moon occupying places of special prominence. It is also possible that persons engaged in certain key trades, such as the working of metal, sought to have periodic interruptions in their labors so that fires might cool and due reverence be rendered to the powers behind the gift of fire and iron.[1]

Explanations of the origin and special meaning of the Sabbath Day have been made in association with the above ancient Near Eastern realities. None of them suffices. Nor does the simple division of sacred time into periods of seven offer a sufficient explanation, although that explanation does have particular weight. The problem is that the introduction of the observance of one day in seven upon which no work is to be done is an act that seems not to be tied precisely to the movement of the planets, the alternation of the seasons, or the organization of the community for the exchange of goods. As the commandment now appears, at any rate, it simply flattens out the days into multiples of seven and requires that the seventh in the repeated series be set aside for rest. No regular work is to be done on that seventh day.

The two dominant explanations as to why no work is to be done are found in the two versions of the Decalogue, in Exod. 20: 11 and in Deut. 5:15. According to the long verse in Exodus, God rested on the seventh day after having created heaven and earth and all that is in them. As God rested and hallowed the seventh day, so also human beings are to do the same (see Gen. 2:2–3). The explanation in Deuteronomy is quite different. Human beings need rest, and especially do servants need rest. Israel is to remember that she served in Egypt as a servant, and God brought deliverance from servanthood. So also the slaves or servants of human beings, at least one day in seven, must know that God does not condemn human beings to slavery forever. Exodus stresses the theological point that God arranged time in such a way as to build sacred rest into the very structure of the creation. Deuteronomy underscores the social-ethical need for human beings to have rest from grinding labor. The human being is not just an instrument, a tool, and labor is not all that human beings are made for.[2]

Neither of these explanations is likely to be of great antiquity. In all probability, however, the observance of the Sabbath is of great antiquity indeed. The observance is much older than the explanations of the observance, as is customarily the case.

How are we to account for the decision taken in Israel's early history to set aside one day in seven upon which no work is to be done? I know of no satisfactory explanation. As noted above, there are difficulties with all the customary explanations. Among the most plausible of the recent explanations is the elaborate notion, presented by Hans-Joachim Kraus,[3] that multiples of seven are common in West Semitic cultural and religious practices and that from the cycle of seven probably developed the notion of multiples of seven days between the early spring harvest of the barley and the later harvest of the wheat. Moreover, given the practice of taking note cultically of the passage of seven years, as in the Ugaritic literature and cult, we could have had develop a sense that sacred time tended to divide into such multiples of seven. Then, under the influence of the lunar month, which roughly divided the lunar month into four units of seven, the Israelites slowly developed their recognition of a seven-day week. And the decision to do no work on the seventh would have corresponded, in this view, with the cultic practice of doing no work on the beginning or the ending of the feast cycles of the barley and the wheat harvests.

Eduard Nielsen[4] suggests that the practice of doing no labor on the seventh day may have developed among the Kenite ironworkers of the southern Sinai, among whom Moses lived for some time as an exile from Egypt. Periodic resting of the fires would have been necessary physically for the smiths and could well have been understood as an act of homage to the god of the fire. Perhaps again the symbol of the moon and its four phases would have contributed to the division of time into periods of seven, which then the smiths would have observed regularly and religiously, resting themselves and the fires for the working of the metal every seventh day.

We require, if we can find it, some explanation of the origin of the seventh day as a day of rest that will account for its flying in the face of any of the regular rhythms of the season or of the heavenly bodies. That is what is so remarkable about the appearance of the Sabbath—the fact that it ignores all normal rhythms. Feast days may or may not fall on the Sabbath; according to ancient Israelite custom, at any rate, the movement of the Sabbath takes precedence over the appearance of the New Year's day, the three agricultural festivals, and all the rest. Later, sectarian groups will worry about such a fact and will try to organize the calendar so that the feast days and the Sabbath Day miss one another. But that development shows only how old the observance of one day in seven, irrespective of the seasons or the movement of the astral bodies, actually was.

It is noteworthy that the Hebrew Bible offers no specifications as to what one is in fact to do on the Sabbath. Only very sparse regulations of what is *not* to occur on the Sabbath Day appear in the canonical Old Testament, although later legislation will fill in the picture for the community. Fundamentally, the seventh day is rightly observed when the community stops doing what it normally does and ceases from labor. The seventh day must then have been understood as some kind of taboo day, a day on which no work was to be done for fear of giving offense to Yahweh. But why would Yahweh demand cessation from all labor on one day in seven? We saw that our two explanations given in the additions to the two versions of the Decalogue are both late. Even so, taken together, they give us an explanation not likely to be too far from the intention of the ancient legislation.

We saw that the first three commandments stake out a claim on the part of God to the exclusive loyalty of the community. Yahweh is to have no rivals. No plastic image of him can be made. No misuse of the power inherent in the name is permitted. Now we have a commandment that flatly prohibits the devotion of the community to meeting its physical needs with no thought of Yahweh. Every seventh day the community is to recognize that it is God who sees to the community's needs, that it is not able fully to care for itself. No matter how successfully the community might be able to till the soil or care for the flocks or regulate trade or develop divisions of labor and trade and commerce, it must bear in mind that it is Yahweh who sees to the organization of the community's life. Every seventh day the community must stop what it normally does, stop the normal provision for its own needs. It must cease all the realities that are involved in human beings' caring for their lives and the lives of those in their charge—in terms of mere physical needs.

Where could such an understanding have arisen? It must have arisen in a community in which people had come to discover their radical dependence upon the transcendent God, but in such a way as not to leave them with a sense of impotence or helplessness in face of this God. It must have involved an understanding of the power of the Holy that required at one and the same time a good deal of self-reliance, a strong sense of the value of work in the world and of the significance of the personal labor of the community and its individual members, together with a sense of the limits of what human beings could do for themselves. But that is simply to suggest that the requirement not to labor on the seventh day may have come from the man Moses, as did the insistent demands that God have no rivals, that no images of him be made, and that his name not be used to do mischief or violence to others. The seventh day is to be Yahweh's day in a special way: it will serve as Yahweh's gift back to the living beings who on the seventh day can enjoy rest from grinding labor.

It seems likely that the Sabbath was set aside by Moses in some dependence upon practices already observed in the Midianite-Kenite culture. We know from Exodus 18 that Moses was ready to listen to the counsel of his father-in-law with regard to the organization of the tribal structures. There, too, the number ten (and multiples of ten) appears, rather than the number twelve, the number of the tribal groups. Multiples of ten are hard to explain in connection with the organization of the families of Israel for judgment and for warfare, just as the organization of the days into multiples of seven, leading to the introduction of the Sabbath, is hard to explain. It could well be that the tradition is right in associating the first with Jethro and the second with Moses in the land of Jethro.

The significance in ancient Israel of the observance of the seventh day as a day of rest from all labor is hard to assess. During the period prior to the Maccabean uprising we hear of no instances in which the people are brought to grief because of their refusal to do battle on the seventh day. Nor do we learn of the observance of the Sabbath as occasion for the foreign nations to look upon Israel in amazement for their oddities of religious practice, as later the Romans occasionally do. Could it be, then, that the strict observance of the seventh day as a day of rest belongs to a later period in Israel's history? Or might the absence of such references simply mean that in the ancient world prior to the Syrian campaigns of the second century before the Common Era there was a greater readiness to respect the religious traditions of peoples in conducting warfare? It would appear from such a reference as 2 Sam. 11:1 that there were agreed-upon conventions as to when warfare was to be waged; it may also be that there were widespread ways of accepting taboo days of the enemy and avoiding them (if not because of respect for the enemy traditions, then out of fear that a violation of the taboo might bring evil consequences upon the offender).

That the observance of the seventh day as a taboo day made the Sabbath a religious day ought not to be doubted, as some scholars have done. Cessation from the normal and ordinary pursuits of life was not merely one of the social conventions that developed into a matter of great social-ethical significance, as one scholar has claimed.[5] It was a division of time, a permanent division, and thus for that reason alone it was very important religiously and cultically, even if the early tradition did not specify what sorts of acts of religious observance belonged on that day. As a day set apart for Yahweh as "holy to the Lord," its basic observance was negatively put: do not do any kind of labor! A community that recognizes that one day out of seven belongs to God and that the way to give it to God is to stop doing what one ordinarily does—break with the grasping for food and shelter and a better life, break with all efforts to secure one's place in the world, break with even the normal acts of cult and pilgrimage —such a community knows that life consists of more than work, more than food, more than shelter, more than protection from one's enemies, more than religious rites and sacrifice and prayer.[6]

It is the absence of religious duties to be performed on the Sabbath that makes the day so striking. One grim story from the Book of Numbers relates how a person was stoned to death for daring to gather sticks on the Sabbath (Num. 15:32–36). But nowhere do we find specifications of what ought positively to be done on the Sabbath. Traditions will develop that explain the way in which the Sabbath is to be observed; my grandfather was never in any doubt as to how his grandchildren were to observe the Sabbath from morning until evening. But nothing is more impressive than this constraint in dealing with the requirements of Sabbath observance.

Rest, it is clear, is just as important as work. Indeed, it would seem that the definition of work ought to be secured by reference to rest, rather than the other way around. Work is a cessation from rest, a claiming of time for the maintenance and preservation of life that is characteristic of life outside the Garden of Eden. The first man and woman, of course, did work in the garden, tending it and caring for it (Gen. 2:15). Indeed, they were placed there to do so, but they were created before the garden was created; they were not made first and foremost for work. That is to say, the human being has a meaning in life that is fundamentally beyond the identification of the human being with labor to be performed. Humankind is *homo ludens* indeed, but that is not the first identification of the human being. The first "work" done by the male formed by God was to compose some lines of poetry with which to greet the gift of the woman shaped from his rib (Gen. 2:23). The couple comes into being in order that each may contribute life to the other, that life may be shared, that aloneness may be overcome. In that setting, work emerges, with life intended (according to the first story of the Creation in Gen. 1:1—2:4a) to involve being fruitful, multiplying, caring for the earth, seeing to its needs. But in neither of the stories of creation is work looked upon as the reason the human being was called into being. Companionship with God and with one another marks the life of the first couple in the garden. Care for the earth is a responsibility falling upon human beings, male and female, as a part of God's blessing, God's *berakhah,* not as a result of the curse of God. Work follows upon a larger and more basic purpose of God. God intends that human beings act in relationship to the divine blessing, find the fulfillment of their lives in the world where they have been placed, both by working and more particularly by resting from work.[7]

This commandment would surely appear to have little import for human beings today. The tasks we face in most Western societies involve less and less physical or even mental labor on the part of human beings and more and more responsibility to find ways to use the time available to humankind in productive and fulfilling endeavors. A commandment not to be preoccupied with labor but to find regular occasions for rest would seem to be the last kind of commandment we need in most countries today. But is the matter that straightforward and simple?

For one thing, the very need to understand and to interpret leisure and the opportunities provided for retired persons, as the span of life increases, is tied up with an understanding of this ancient commandment. If labor is to be understood in relation to rest, then we can underscore the point that the retired or the unemployed person has, on this score, no reason to see life as meaningless. No, the question is rather how the time available might serve the purposed ends of God in the world. That is no simple question to answer, but it is a question that applies both to those who work and to those who are retired, to those with work and to those without work. How do employed persons use the time they have, on and off the job, to serve God's purposed ends for them? How do those who have been retired from normal labor or those who have lost jobs or those who have never as yet had a proper job use the time available to them in light of God's purposes? We can say that God probably intends all persons to have meaningful and fulfilling work. Thus the human community cannot accept situations in which people, young or not so young, seek employment in order to find fulfillment in work and also to earn their living but can find no work. The fourth commandment should not be understood to call into question the meaningfulness or the normal necessity of work.

Even so, as machines and other contrivances reduce the need for certain kinds of work by human beings in the world, the opportunity will come all the more frequently for us to see work in the light of leisure and in the light of how human life finds its fundamental fulfillment not necessarily in direct connection with human labor of the sort we are accustomed to. We can probably come to an understanding of such situations only when they actually confront us. But already many more persons than ever before are having to find purpose for their lives in very loose connection with labor performed or to be performed.

Of enormous importance in this connection is the discovery by many people that they have time to be volunteer workers in behalf of fellow human beings and in ways that will not threaten the rights or the opportunities of salaried persons. As the life of Western peoples gets ever more depersonalized, active efforts to introduce humane and personal dimensions into our bureaucracies and other aspects of the common life are needed. Older persons can be regularly associated with the quite young—in day-care centers, kindergartens, schools, playgrounds—for the good of both groups. Normal services such as the postal service, care for the cleanliness and beauty of our towns and villages, care for hospitals, schools, prisons, libraries, and many other institutions of organized social existence apparently cannot function smoothly or with a commitment to humaneness. The available unemployed or underemployed offer an excellent resource for helping in these areas; so also do retired persons. Salaries may be called for, but they need not be full salaries and they need not be given in such a way as to do injustice to persons fully salaried.

The point is that many of the persons who would be taking up this kind of work would do so from a position of current leisure or underemployment. In taking such jobs, they could be helped to see that, apart from the personal satisfaction from being employed and from the work itself, their work clearly has a dimension of service to fellow human beings.

In addition to the need to understand leisure and to do so in relation to the commandment not to work on the seventh day, people today need to discover how to find joy in the work that they actually do. That too depends on a right understanding of the fourth commandment.

Work in the Bible is understood to be a part of one's service in the care of God's good earth. The work done in the world includes work in the temple precincts and prayers and praises at the temple, which are a part of our *'abōdāh,* or service, to God. The Book of Proverbs enjoins persons to do their work and do it well, not being slothful or sloppy in labor.[8] It is assumed that every person has work to do, that God counts on human beings to struggle with the earth so it may yield its treasures, and that members of the family will carry their respective shares of the load of work that must be done.

But there is no glorification of work. Work is not made out to be something so enriching and fulfilling for human beings that when it is properly done or properly understood it will always give pleasure to the worker. There is indeed a limited connection drawn in Genesis 3 between sin and labor, although it does not seem to mean that work is itself sinful. Rather, the point is that human beings have spoiled the relationship they have with God, with one another, and with God's other creatures as a result of the sin committed in the garden, and that all they do is thereby affected for ill.

People must work, then, so that the earth will yield its goods and so that life will support the human community. They can take pleasure in work, but they are not taught in the Bible that they should do so. Human beings do their work in a matter-of-fact way. The connection drawn between the planting of the fields, the harvesting, the tilling of the soil, and the care of trees and vines on the one hand, and the bounty of these, their productivity, on the other hand, is treated in the Bible without any resort to what we might call a sexual or an ecstatic connection between such work and its results. In the religions surrounding the biblical world, such a connection between work and ecstasy or work and sexuality was widely drawn, and it did give a special impetus to work. In the act of agriculture or in fulfilling the pastoral vocation, one was engaged in a religious and a ritual act. The biblical world takes away such an understanding, and labor is thereby desacralized. There is loss in such a desacralization, of course, but there also is great gain.

But how is there to be any real joy in work if the desacralization is insisted upon? The joy comes in relation to doing the will of God, finding one's place in the world, and fulfilling that place. One's place includes a place of work, a commitment to a part of the world's work that is one's own responsibility. But all ideological notions of workers united against owners, or workers caught up in a great international community of those who earn their living by labor rather than by the enjoyment of life as capitalist or exploiter, must be viewed with suspicion. It is easy to romanticize labor, and despite the undoubted good that has come from such romanticization in the course of the development of labor movements, such romanticism should be seen for what it is. In our kind of world there is no longer any basis for finding sufficient joy in labor alone. The joy in work must come as a part of joy in life, joy in the living of a worthwhile and meaningful life.

And that is where, once again, the Sabbath comes into its own. In ancient times the seventh day provided time for persons to reflect on the story of God's work, on the meaning of their lives. It provided a time for children to hear about the history of Israel from parents and grandparents and other family members. It provided time for the family and the community jointly to take responsibility for the sharing of those elements of the tradition to which meaning attached itself in special ways, and the result was that the Sabbath offered a way for the identification of those who constituted this people Israel.

Under right circumstances Sunday has served the same end for Christians and for the Christian community. Over time, however, in our contemporary world, the days set aside for worship and meditation and other days of rest, as well as the days normally appointed for work, do not carry much weight of this sort. Parents often blame the school system for not providing their children with the traditions and values of the society, while the school authorities rightly point out that there is barely sufficient time or expertness simply to help young persons come to terms with the subject matter thought to be essential at each stage of preparation for later study and for earning a living, entering upon one's planned vocation. How can the embattled schools find opportunity to reflect with young persons on the meaning of life?

But the parents who both have to work in order to maintain the home, who are caught up in further studies in order that the work they do may prosper and their professional advancement proceed, and who need some time for their own adult preoccupations, also do not have time to transmit the heritage and help the young reflect upon its meaning.

What about synagogue and church? Can they provide what home and school seem no longer able to offer? That is a possibility not to be overlooked, but it would call for a radical re-orientation of the work of synagogue and church, with the greater changes perhaps required within Christian congregational organization. Some may indeed despair over the prospect, and that for two reasons. Not only would the costs be enormous with regard to the reorientation of the clergy and the rearrangement of staff and support for staff, but the danger of indoctrination would be immense, as we can see from the practice of certain synagogues and churches already, where the effort to do just what is called for is being carried out, but with an ideological tenacity that is, if anything, more alarming than the loss of any sense of values or the loss of time to reflect on life's meaning with the young.

What is called for is the designation of one day out of seven as a day for just this kind of task. That is perhaps utopian in itself, but it needs to be thought about. Were it possible for us to say that among the great religions there is agreement that such a time is needed, and any society is well advised to provide it, that would be the precondition for such a provision of one day in seven for reflection upon the meaning of our common life on the part of all citizens. As things now stand, it would be entirely possible for us to have a day set aside for Jewish reflection and worship (the Jewish Sabbath), another for Christian worship and reflection (the Christian Sunday), and, where necessary, another for Muslim worship and reflection (the Islamic Friday). The four-day week would thus be Monday through Thursday, and labor on four days would well suffice in many countries already, with a smaller group of persons in effect keeping the communities' essential functions in operation on those three days.

Such a situation already obtains to some extent in the state of Israel, where these lines are being written. It is far from the case, however, that the three days nominally available for worship and reflection are being satisfactorily used for such purposes— as all persons of my acquaintance would agree. The framework is there; that is all.

It may be that some adjustments as to how the respective days are to be reserved for such worship and reflection will be necessary. It seems unfair, for example, for Sundays to be regular days

of work for all persons who do not register their religious conviction against work on Sunday, just as it seems unfair for Satur-
day to be a regular workday for all who do not insist that religion
prevents such work. A society needs to work out such a system
of time away from normal pursuits that both the need for time
and reflection and the increasing need for physical exercise in
group sports as well as for participating in such sports as specta-
tors will all be possible.

Given the time, the synagogues and churches and mosques and
other religious bodies can begin to claim such time and find ways
to make its use genuinely productive. That will by no means be
a simple matter. It needs to be done with the support of the secular authorities, even though they may well feel that such activities belong to religious communities. The secular state should no
longer be so shortsighted as to hold to such a view. Prudence
dictates its support of any effort that offers even a remote possibility of helping the citizenry recover or develop a wholesome
sense of values, an understanding or a set of understandings of
the meaning of human life on the planet, and a series of ways to
assure that the younger generation gives serious time and thought
to these. Look, for example, at the utter breakdown of most
bureaucracies, at the inability of police to do anything significant
to diminish the increasing crime rate, at the widespread corruption of business morality and the loss of integrity in society generally, and at the increasing violence, brutality, and contempt for
the life, welfare, and goods of others. Can any society begrudge
the resources needed to give opportunity for religious communities to attempt, on their own initiatives and in their own ways,
to deal with the meaning of life in society today?

The introduction of the observance of one day in seven for
rest, for the cessation from work, once brought about remarkable
social changes—in ancient Israel. The prophetic checks upon
kingship in ancient Israel are unthinkable apart from time to reflect on the dangers of political power in the hands of one person.
The development of hymns and laments that identify the actual
course of life under God and are brutally frank in their portrayal
of how life often gets out of control, or appears to do so, is also

hard to imagine apart from the observance of the Sabbath Day. And so is the teaching of Jesus, or the development of Mishnah and Gemara for the Jewish community. The Sabbath was a time when one could ponder the actual course of life, see to its difficulties and dangers as well as its joys and opportunities. One might therefore say that, apart from the Sabbath Day, we might well not have had the other commandments in the Decalogue.

THE FIFTH COMMANDMENT:
NO CONTEMPT FOR THE FAMILY
"THOU SHALT NOT CURSE THY
FATHER OR THY MOTHER"

The second of the two tables is often said to begin with the commandment to honor parents. The Sabbath law already focuses attention upon human life and the needs of animals as well as human beings for rest and refreshment. With the fifth commandment, requiring respect for parents, we seem to leave the realm of religious-theological understandings and enter the world of social and family relations. Such an effort to divide the commandments into contents suitable for two different tables is probably without justification, however. It may well be that originally the reference to the two tables was understood to mean the production of two identical exemplars of the one set of commandments, as noted above.

The showing of respect for parents is a common theme in the Old Testament. Children are encouraged to be obedient and are indeed subject to most severe penalties should they not yield to the wishes of father and mother (Deut. 21:18–21). To be a rebellious son is to have no place in the community of God's people. It would appear that the Old Testament in this respect offers counsel that is outmoded and in fact ought to be rejected as pernicious. We know well enough how parents can tyrannize their children, crush their spirits, and do damage, the effects of which may continue to the end of life. This commandment, therefore, may be one that should simply be ignored in contemporary life, although of course a proper respect for parents is certainly to be taught to children.

It would be rash, however, to assume too quickly that the commandment, either in its presumed negative form as given above or in the positive form found in the Hebrew text, meant to bend the will of the children to that of the parents. Our Decalogue is directed first of all to *adults,* to the adult male members of the community of Israel. Younger members of the community are not excluded, but they are certainly not the focus of attention.

The persons addressed are adults, but are young adults more in view than older ones? Or rather, are the parents in question still giving basic guidance to their children, teaching them how adults are to comport themselves, or are they *older* parents whom the (adult) children might treat with contempt because of their age, frailty, or backwardness? The alternatives may not be exclusive, but much depends upon where the emphasis falls. We believe that this commandment, like the others, has the adult members of the community clearly and prominently in view. Therefore, the commandment would be misunderstood if it were thought of as designed to keep young children in line, to keep them tractable and dutiful and respectful of their elders.

The connection between the fourth and the fifth commandments may be the clearer if we recognize that the commandment focused on the treatment of aged parents by the mature members of the community. Just as human beings and beasts need rest from their labors, and just as grinding toil does not constitute the only reason for human life and activity, so also human beings do not cease to have worth and significance when the time for their productive working years has run its course. Parents are to be respected and cared for in their time of feebleness, diminished activity, or senility. When they enter upon their "sabbath" rest they are to be shown respect and honor such as they were shown in their time of active membership in the community. Interpreted in this way, the commandment then follows well upon that devoted to the regulation of the flow of time.

But do we have an adequate justification for the use of the strong Hebrew term *qll*? Is it the same as cursing father or mother to show contempt for them in their old age? Here the occurrence of the two participially formed laws in Exod. 21:15

and 17 may be of help. The first, 21:15, provides the death penalty for anyone who strikes father or mother. The action in view is certainly that of a young and truculent teenage son who will no longer yield obedience to parents—such action as is specified all the more clearly in Deut. 21:18–21. The second of these passages has something beyond the use of abusive language in view. To curse one's father or mother means to treat them as of no consequence or value, to wish them removed from the scene, to desire their obliteration. And that suggests that the parents are aged or frail and have become a nuisance to the active adults who would very much like to be relieved of further responsibility for such aged ones.

It is in this connection that the prophetic power of the commandment emerges. In this connection there also appears the problematic character of any attempt to use this commandment to enforce care for aged parents in our own generation, for our generation has learned well the ambiguity of the relations of parents to children and of children to parents. It is an enormously complex relationship, perhaps the most complex of all human relationships, not excluding that between husband and wife. So much depends upon this relation, and in so many ways, that the issues inherent in the fifth commandment are particularly sensitive and difficult to sort out and state rightly.

The relations between parents and children are of immense importance for the health of human beings and for the family, as Freud saw. Since Freud's time, many and varied studies of these relations by psychiatrists, psychotherapists of many sorts, psychologists, social anthropologists, and sociologists have produced a vast literature and many approaches to how such relations can be made mutually supportive and wholesome. The connection between the generation of the parents and that of the children may have its most overt points of tension as the children become teenagers, but the problems between the generations do not disappear in later years. One of the areas of very grave concern is that when the parents have grown old they become to some extent dependent upon their adult children, thus reversing the dependency roles of the earlier teenage years. Now it is the parents who may feel resentment that they can no longer control their own destinies.

The addition made to the presumed original form of the commandment shows that long life is the matter in question. If one wishes to enjoy long life, one needs to see to the life of one's parents when the time for doing so arrives. God promises a long and full life to the righteous, but such a full set of days is not assured. It is the lot in store for human beings, but with a given number of years—threescore and ten, according to Psalm 90— also stands the inevitability of death. It is well-known that the Hebrew Bible, at least until quite late in Israel's history, offers little hope of meaningful life beyond the grave. Such continuity as is available comes through the continued existence of the people of the promise; Israel exists through time until the Day of the Consummation, but the individual Israelite is mortal and marked for death.

Just in this setting, however, stands our commandment. It calls upon every human being to refrain from any action that would denigrate the life and worth of human beings who have lost much of their "commercial" worth, and in particular those human beings on whom one's own life has depended. Even when due allowance is made for the changed situation between the times of ancient Israel and our own times, this understanding is a striking one. Granted, traditional societies have frequently developed in such a way as to give value and dignity to old age: with work entrusted to the aged, with advice sought from them in certain areas of life, and with changing functions marked out into which one may easily move as one ages. Even so, it is clear from many biblical references that the father was in many cases not willing to relinquish leadership to the son at the appropriate time. In the most notable Old Testament instance, David refused to designate a successor to himself as king of Israel, a fateful delay that very nearly produced yet another revolution within the family of David (see 1 Kings 1). And according to the chronology of the Books of Kings, Rehoboam was forty-one years of age before he was able to succeed his father Solomon on the throne. He seems to have been ill-fitted to assume this responsibility and made incredibly foolish decisions immediately upon coming to the throne (1 Kings 12).

While such instances are special in that the persons in question are kings or sons of kings, the same situation certainly must have been of common occurrence. Given large families, and given the attachment to the land that was impressed upon the youth of ancient Israel, many a son of Israel must have suffered for years the need to çontinue dutifully to follow the wishes of the father, even when those wishes were unwise or unsound. It is one of the features of senility that those who have become senile often cannot be persuaded that their capacities have in fact diminished.

There probably was, then, ample reason for the commandment to honor father and mother or to withhold the curse against them or to refuse to treat them with the disdain or anger one felt. And why not? Must we not say that the commandment is outmoded in that it calls for the enslavement of the current generation to the arbitrary wishes of the older generation? Such an arrangement invites traditionalism, a refusal to change or to learn from fresh understandings and discoveries. The older generation is surely entitled to life and such comfort of life, to dignity and continuing respect and wholesome engagements in life, as can be provided by the active generation. But the latter need not, on the strength of this biblical commandment, forfeit its own rights and remain in the thralldom of a generation that has had its opportunity for life and creativity.

Is there not likely to be a dimension to this commandment greater than the admonition to care for the older generation when it has lived out most of its useful days? I believe that there is. The honoring of parents is the honoring of those who have seen to one's own life from its very beginnings. Here, too, the differences between our own times and those of the Bible must not be overlooked. In ancient societies the more wealthy parents had servants to assist at the time of childbearing and as the children were being reared and educated. The burden of rearing children often fell less heavily upon the two parents in such instances; members of the extended family were also present to lend support and guidance. But in ancient times the responsibility for the care of children extended over a much longer period than it does today. Parents held on to this responsibility longer, but the community also saw to it that they did. They did not lay aside their parental responsibilities when the children reached a certain age.

In any case, despite the differences, ancient Israelite society knew, as does our own society, that there is a connection between the lives of parent and child that is so deep and fateful that its influence upon both can hardly be overestimated. The generations are tied together by the giving of love and care and by the receiving of love and care in the bond of the family. To curse mother and father is thus an enormity that cannot be endured. It is a cursing of love itself, of life itself, a cursing, indeed, of oneself. Much worse than acts of physical violence against the parents is the violence of the curse. The dishonoring of mother and father means the attacking of the very springs and sources of life itself. How can one curse one's own parents without being drawn into the vortex of destruction of one's own children? The contempt shown to those one has depended upon will surely be felt by those who in their turn depend upon the contempt-showing parents.

At this juncture, however, the changes in family life that are occurring with such rapidity in the Western world need to be called to our attention. Since "parenting" is itself such a complex issue, and since new patterns of marriage and life together are developing within Western and other societies, is the time not at hand to seek alternatives to such a bondedness in love—and hate —as family life often entails? Were that possible, it might be unnecessary to fret about this commandment, which is already recognizable as one of the most dubious of the ten.

Whether the tyranny of relations between parent and child can be broken by some of the newer approaches to family life and the rearing of children, such as the kibbutz or other collective family arrangements, remains to be seen. It would be rash to count on the development of any forms of life together that will eliminate the tie, for good and for ill, that exists between parent and child. And there is no difficulty whatever in our identifying forms of family relationship that are more healthy than other forms, or in seeing how the commandment against the cursing of mother and father can still function effectively today.

In this instance, as in most of those to follow, the continuing applicability of the commandment to daily life is not to be seen as direct or literal. What is it that this commandment, in its negative form, wished most to safeguard in the life of ancient Israel? We have maintained that it was not intended primarily to support the parents in their disciplining of unruly children. It had in view, rather, the care of the aged, the treatment of old parents with dignity and thoughtfulness by their adult children. That commandment continues to have its weight, although it would be wrong and wicked for us quickly to suggest that some of the presently used alternatives for caring for aged parents are instances of "cursing" father and mother, for example, placing them in nursing homes, visiting them infrequently. No, the import of a commandment to care for aged parents and not to treat them with contempt finds applicability today in much more subtle ways. Who can really be sure whether it is a kindness or a curse to keep the elderly in one's own home when they are not able to cope with the normal demands of life in such a home and must appear more and more to the other members of the household as unfit, incapable of managing life? In such a circumstance, the very conditions of life in the home contribute to the feeling that the parents are an object of pity if not of contempt. The vaunted blessings of having the elderly parents on hand to share life with the grandchildren, and thus of bridging the generations, may well be lost in this unwholesome situation.

On the other hand, it is unmistakable that life in our contemporary society often is immensely enriched by the presence of the elder parents within the home. The children have their ambivalence toward their parents, but their children are spared much of that and simply know the delights of having persons devoted to them, members of the family, who have time and are interested and can share life with them to a degree often impossible for the parents. And the children can learn from their association with the grandparents to appreciate the life that they, in their day, shared with their parents, thereby coming to appreciate more what is involved in the bearing and rearing of children. Keeping the elderly parents close to the other members of the family may, then, be one of the most effective ways of engendering real respect for parents, one of the most effective checks against treating the elderly with contempt.

One other dimension of this commandment's import is more implicit than explicit. In the ancient Near Eastern world the parent-child relationship was widely used as an image of the God-and-people relationship. Although widespread, there is in Exod. 4:22–23 evidence of a quite early application of this imagery to Yahweh and Israel, and in a context of great intimacy, beyond the familiar usage in the other societies of the ancient world. The commandment to honor parents, or to withhold the curse from them, is probably affected by the use of parent-child language for the relation of Yahweh and Israel, as is unmistakable in a later period (Hosea, Jeremiah). The admonition not to curse father or mother, then, is motivated in part by the recognition of the analogy between human parents and the deity as father or mother to Israel. To be sure, the firm insistence upon the unity of God that comes with the first commandment will mean that the analogy cannot function as it so often did and does in various religions: a divine pair bringing their divine son (Osiris-Isis-Horus, e.g.), the actual world-ruler, into active relation with the world. For Israel the analogy can, within acceptable theological understanding, go no further than the conferral of a special respect upon the parents who have been co-creators of life along with God. And it is evident that even to that extent a danger was sensed, for the explanation added to this commandment by the later tradition stresses not this connection of the child's life with its human "creators" but the connection of long life on the part of the parents with a long life that the children may enjoy if they faithfully see to the needs of those who bore them.

It is difficult to know just how important this element of the divine dimension of parenting was in ancient Israel. One thing seems certain: the Israelites well knew the mystery of the bondage one generation feels to the preceding and the following generations. There are few mysteries deeper in the social existence of humankind. In it is included the mystery of humankind as sexual. One knows that one's life is interwoven with the life of father and of mother. One knows also that one's life is interwoven with the life of children, but there seems to be an especially deep ambivalence on the part of children toward their parents, due in large measure, no doubt, to the way in which life and adulthood have to be striven for and seized, sometimes at the expense of the life and selfhood of the parents. How is the one generation to succeed the present one? What are the rules? What is permitted and what is ruled out in principle? We know that there are societies that had no compunction about exposing unwanted children, and that there are societies that had no compunction about leaving the aged exposed to die when they were no longer able to fend for themselves. Neither is permissible in Israel, and neither was permissible in ancient Egypt, Mesopotamia, Canaan, or Asia Minor, not as a matter of course. For Israel, the cursing of parents or any mistreatment of them was subject to the death penalty, as was (according to late Deuteronomic legislation perhaps never fully enforced) rebelliousness on the part of sons or daughters. Underscoring this fifth commandment, then, is Israel's insistence that the adult Israelite cannot secure freedom from father or mother at the expense of humiliating, cursing, or doing away with either of them. On the contrary, if the Israelite expects his or her own life to flourish, it will be necessary for such a one to bear in mind that in Yahweh's eyes one condition for such flourishing is precisely how the elderly parents are treated.

Once again we see how this body of ancient guidance for Israel worked to govern relations within the family, the larger community, and the cult as well. One is prohibited from striking out to secure freedom for oneself as an adult by doing damage to those who up to now have been entrusted with one's freedom—the parents. One is prevented from using the power of the curse against parents who mysteriously exercise a special rule over one, just as one is prevented from using the power of invoking God's name to do damage to anyone in the community, thereby infringing upon the very power of Yahweh himself. The relations between parents and children are not to be of a sort that holds children in thralldom to tyrannical parents. Every generation has to find its life and freedom over against the parents, and that is still an enormously complex social difficulty.

Nothing is said here about the complex relations spelled out in such detail in Deuteronomy 27 governing sexual dealings within the family. The Decalogue concentrates all its attention just here—on the relations between the two generations. And there is no doubt, I believe, that this was a stroke of genius. Laws governing sexual relations within the family have much of their function in the managing of just what is involved in the relations between parents and children. True, specifications will be necessary to indicate the limits of marriage relations, but much of the curse ritual discussed above has in view not marriage but the overstepping of the sexual boundaries within the family, and thus is an extension of the issue of the relation between parents and children. With the prohibition of misdealings of the children with their parents the Decalogue can leave entirely to one side these grave sexual crimes, crimes that must have filled the community with horror when it saw them. The expression "Such a thing ought not to be done in Israel," which we find especially in association with such sexual crimes, and the identification of such crimes as "wanton folly," reveal the abhorrence felt by the community over violations of the sexual taboos.[9]

Our commandment leaves aside all those issues and incorporates them under the heading of the cursing of father and mother. In this way the authority of the parents is affirmed and reinforced, but the commandment aims at much more than underscoring parental discipline of children and parental leadership within the society; the focal issue is the generations and their interconnection, and that problem is even more complex for a society to manage than the problem of sibling rivalry. How is the child to move from complete dependence upon the parents to a situation in which the same child becomes solely responsible for the very life of the same parents? How can the necessary changes along the way from birth to old age and death be accomplished? What force and what set of strictures can control the virtually unlimited and therefore potentially demonic power of parents over children in early years? And what force or set of conventions can assure that when adult children reach a position of overweening power within the community they will not repay parents for the abuse of power in earlier years?

The commandment does not say, "Love your father and your mother." It is content, in the presently received form, to call for giving honor or respect to the parents, and in the presumed earlier form to insist upon the avoidance of the curse or of treatment with contempt. Certainly the Israelite community would have wished to see its members treat all persons with due and proper respect, showing dishonor or contempt to none. But the situation of the (elderly) parents is particularly difficult, for the parents will have given ample cause to the children to return evil for evil received. The commandment prohibits this claiming of one's own from the parents when the opportunity comes, and therein lies its great moral and human force. Just as Yahweh took care of infant Israel when she was a child and entirely helpless (e.g., Ezek. 16), so earthly parents spend themselves for the children. And in many an instance the reward received is what Yahweh also received, according to Ezekiel: contemptuous disregard, violation of all bonds of loyalty. It must not be so.

Thus once again we find a brief, pungent, originally negative statement of what simply cannot obtain in Israel: father and mother are not to be dishonored. As in the case of the other commandments, nothing is said about how such a commandment is to be made effective within the society. No penalties are stated. No threats appear. Just a laconic sentence sums up one of the most enriching and devastating aspects of the life of human beings upon the earth. Other animals certainly show some features of the bonds that connect the generations to one another, but in no other instances of life together do we find the enormously complex set of associations that govern the relations between human parents and children. It is not too much to say that all other human relations develop in association with those that emerge in the family. If a society can find a way to enable the younger generation to treat the older with due respect, see to its actual needs, show that life and love can be passed on as a gift to those who have themselves in their time been the givers of life and love in two directions—to their elderly parents and also to their own children—then that society has come to terms with one of the most difficult of all social issues. Our commandments say nothing about respect between brother and brother or brother and sister. They say nothing about incest or that driving reality that often destroys relations within the family: lust and hatred that follows upon the yielding to lust (see 2 Samuel 13). The only reality within the family—certainly Israel's central social institution—that requires attention within the Decalogue is the relation between parent and child, between child and parent. If that relation is managed in a wholesome way, much that would otherwise be serious indeed can be understood to be no more than a peccadillo. And if there is real health in the relation of adult parents to their elderly parents, there will be health in the other relations of the family. For it is how one deals with the helpless, with those who can no longer fend for themselves, and with such helpless ones against whom one has a lifetime of grievances for wrongs done or imagined, that provides the test of one's moral and human commitments. Just as the treatment of orphans, widows, and the poor is the general test of justice within the society, so the treatment of elderly parents by their children is the test of family relations as such. And the two are probably very closely related: those who show contempt for the poor, the orphan, and the widow will treat their elderly parents with contempt, and vice versa.

As we look back on the commandment against treating the Sabbath Day lightly and that against showing contempt for one's elderly parents, we can see that we remain in the same general field of thought and feeling. The requirement to set aside one day out of seven for cessation from work reminds us that life consists of more than toil, more than the desperate grubbing for food and shelter and goods, more than the finding of security for ourselves and those dependent upon us. This more has to do

with our having time for reflection on what life is all about, time
for one another, time for God. And in the case of the commandment not to dishonor parents, we once again have to do with a
life that consists of more than production, more than carrying
one's own weight. Life together in the society must be enriched
by regular cessation from labor as well as by labor. Life together in the family must be enriched by the care for one another
even when that care is often a nuisance. Persons grow old and
can no longer carry their share of the family's labors. They cannot simply be discarded, for that would be to curse them, to
treat them with contempt, to forget that these very parents once
cared for us when we were unable to care for ourselves, and
to forget that we shall one day also be dependent upon the care
of our children or their surrogates.

In both instances, therefore, we are dealing with realities of
fundamental importance for the health of the community as a
whole. And in both instances the admonitions govern relations
much wider than those of individuals or families within the community. The keeping of the Sabbath is a matter for the whole
community, although each individual member must be called
upon to do so. The showing of honor for elderly parents is more
particularized, but for its effective working within the community
it too depends upon broad consensus with regard to the treatment
of the elderly. And both these commandments, while capable of
violation by the acts of individuals, aim at overall compliance
by the community. With the next five commandments we have
to do more with individual acts, with particular misdeeds of individuals that would destroy life in community if the acts became rampant, but which can be done, and will be done, by
many individuals within the community without any necessary
threat to the very existence of the community itself. It is possible that the arrangement of the commandments into two groups
of five, one set for each of the two tables and one set for each
of the two hands, had some such recognition in view. Violation
of commandments on either of the two lists is fatefully serious.
But the first prohibitions are such that the community simply
cannot survive for long if it violates them; greater latitude in

terms of sheer survival exists in the case of the acts prohibited by the second table. But the damage to the individuals directly involved in the acts of the second table may well be the more immediate and devastating in their consequences. Both, then, are equally serious sets of prohibitions, but they are serious in distinguishable ways.

CHAPTER 5

Basic Human Obligations

THE SIXTH COMMANDMENT:
NO CONTEMPT FOR HUMAN LIFE
"THOU SHALT NOT TAKE THE LIFE
OF THY NEIGHBOR"

Our reconstruction of the sixth commandment is somewhat different from that proposed by a number of scholars. The nearest equivalents to the commandment are found in Deut. 27:24 and Exod. 21:12. The first of these is probably the older. It uses the same verb found in the second passage, the term *nkh,* to strike or to smite. Exodus 21:12 makes it clear that the struck person in fact will have died before the death penalty obtains. The Deuteronomy passage has the addition of the term "in secret," thus keeping this list of curses focused upon the kinds of crimes that can be done without the community's having knowledge of the crimes.

At first reading the commandment is surprising because of its sweeping generality. The generality is increased if we accept as original the present form of the commandment: thou shalt not kill. But even in our somewhat longer reconstructed form the commandment is surprising in its scope. The Hebrew Bible makes clear from quite early texts that the human community is to be prepared to exercise the death penalty against those who dare to take the life of another human being. Genesis 9:6 seems to be such an ancient law, restricting blood vengeance to the taker of the blood of the victim but giving full warrant, in the

107

case of such a slaying, for the community to exercise the death penalty. And many of the legal collections, as we have seen above, provide for the death penalty in certain instances. Moreover, Yahweh himself, according to the Old Testament, is not at all averse to taking the life of those who grievously violate the commandments or offend against the divine requirements in intolerable ways. There can be no question, therefore, of our sixth commandment's having the initial meaning that human life is never, under any circumstances, to be taken by another human being or by the appointed authorities in Israel.

Moreover, warfare is a regular feature of the life of ancient Israel, with some of the wars declared to be "holy to Yahweh" and to be prosecuted with full confidence that the slaughter of the enemy is ordained by God.[1] Indeed, a failure to exterminate all the enemies is an indication of contempt for Yahweh's requirements and must itself be punished severely. Certain wars are simply a part of life, according to the Old Testament, while others are bidden by God himself and still others are acts of blatant refusal to be obedient to God's will and purposes. But in any event, killing in warfare would seem to be a part of commonly accepted Israelite practice.

Thus there is a killing that is done when someone has taken human life, killing in the form of execution by the community. There is killing that ensues in course of warfare, warfare either permitted by Yahweh or actually ordered by Yahweh. And there is killing as an act of violence against a fellow human being. The problem with our commandment is that it makes none of the above distinctions. Presumably it has in view especially the last-mentioned act of violence against the neighbor. But if so, why did the commandment not make it more clear just how wide-ranging its application was to be? In this instance, the commandment seems to be so sweeping in its coverage as to lose much of its meaning.

But at least we can now say that we have come to a commandment from the ancient list that has direct and immediate applicability to our own day. Such a prohibition is all the more applicable in a time when violence against fellow human beings has become a way of life, violence of such cruelty and apparent senselessness that it defies all rationality and apparently can be met or controlled only with equal application of violence and cruelty against its representatives. "Thou shalt not take the life of thy neighbor." What a commandment for a day in which the life of the neighbor is entirely ours to dispose of for the realization of our own political and ideological purposes!

It was Karl Barth who in recent years best indicated the wide applicability of such a commandment. His treatment of the commandment covers all aspects of the readiness to take human life: murder, capital punishment, war, abortion, euthanasia, forms of birth control, suicide. Under the phrase "reverence for life," Barth, following Albert Schweitzer in the use of the term but not otherwise, showed how a proper respect for life as God's free gift to humankind rules out in principle the taking of human life under any circumstances except those that lie at the very boundary of what is under any possible circumstances permitted to human beings. We shall be using Barth's treatment frequently in what follows.[2] Here the intention is simply to point out what a wide range of human conduct is potentially covered by this simply stated prohibition. It should be noted, however, that if we apply the commandment to all the above aspects of our common life we will enter a thicket of fundamental moral issues facing humankind today, from which there may be no way out!

At the very outset of our discussion of this commandment, we need to acknowledge that for ancient Israel there would have been little difficulty in understanding a distinction often made today and much debated: the distinction between killing that serves the cause of life and killing that does not serve the cause of life. In Gen. 9:6 we have an ancient statement that bears out this point: "Whoever sheds the blood of a human being, by a human being shall that person's blood be shed." The closing clause, "for God made human beings in his own image," is probably a later addition in the style and line of the priestly tradition. According to the ancient poetic couplet, the community is required by God to take human life if someone has dared to do so against God's requirement that human life not be taken.

We should note that this ancient couplet is itself sweeping in its import. No one is to enter into the realm of God's reserved activity, daring to take action where God alone is to act. That is to say, life belongs to God—human life in particular—for God is the author and giver of all of life. Life is sacrosanct, and especially the life of human beings. But how is human life to be preserved? Our text thinks of no other way than the two ways that are here either implicit or stated: (1) that *God* is the author and giver of life, and no one dare act as though that person were God, taking the life of a fellow human being, and (2) that if a person should dare to do so, then in order to hold fast to the commandment that life is sacrosanct and belongs to God alone, the community must act *on God's behalf* to take the life of someone who sheds the blood of a human being.

And therein lies the dilemma that has plagued the human community for centuries: how dare the community claim the right to act on God's behalf? If life belongs to God, what are the circumstances under which any human community can understand itself to be invited by God to act in his place to take the life of another human being?

Great attention has been given to the notion of a "just war"; detailed guidelines have been worked out for the prosecution of warfare held to be warranted by obedience to God's command. But in all such instances it is generally recognized that it must indeed be a grave situation that would issue in a war waged at God's command or at least with the warrant of God. The arguments used in connection with the theory of the "just war" are important for the general issue of taking human life. The entire literature bearing on pacifism and on Christian refusal to do acts of violence against fellow human beings is of course also pertinent to our subject.

All such matters, however, lie beyond the scope of interest of ancient Israel. There the problems with the commandments were grave enough, but they did not lie on the question of whether human life could be taken under any circumstances at all. But why, then, is the commandment stated in such sweeping terms? In every instance thus far our commandments have been of the sort that might be difficult to apply in every imaginable situation in life, thus requiring the development of much additional legislation and the hallowing of many later decisions that then become precedents for the community in subsequent times. But the other commandments have not had such a built-in problem with respect to application, as has this commandment. One who acts in secret to take the life of the neighbor can clearly be called to account by virtue of the solemn curse (Deut. 27:24). One who strikes the neighbor a fatal blow can also be dealt with by application of the death penalty, although in this instance, too, the community will have to inquire concerning the causes and circumstances of the action. But in our commandment there is the seemingly impossible requirement that no one shall take the life of a neighbor, not by any means or for any reasons at all. If we eliminate the object of the killing and use only the current text of Exodus, "Thou shalt not kill," the prohibition is even more comprehensive, so that any act of killing is ruled out in principle. Applied strictly, the commandment would mean that there are absolutely no circumstances that would justify taking the life of any other human being. We have indicated that there is no support in the Old Testament for such a sweeping prohibition: it would appear not to fit the world of the ancient Israelite at all, however appealing such an understanding of the commandment might be to us today. Giving God complete priority, making no images of God, refusing to use God's name to do harm to others, refraining from every kind of labor on the seventh day, and withholding any action to damage the life of one's aged parents—all these actions, difficult as they may be, are in principle commitments that persons can make with the expectation that, with the help of God and of fellow human beings within the community, they will be able to keep them. But what about a commandment not to kill the neighbor? We would have to say that the ancient Israelites must have sensed from the outset that with this commandment we enter a somewhat different realm of human behavior, a different kind of requirement from the God of the covenant.

And through the generations, various societies too have found a touchstone for all moral action in the regulation of the ways in which the life of a human being might be taken by another human being. Once again, then, we can say that there is a logic to the division of the commandments into two groups of five, with the commandment to have no God other than Yahweh leading the first list and the commandment to take no human life leading the second.

The second table, led off by a commandment that makes human life sacrosanct, is not concerned with what is to happen in the case of violations of the prohibitions. Rather, it wishes, as with the first table as well, to underscore kinds of action that would mean the ruin of human life in community. Human beings, the ancient Israelite prophets knew, require for meaningful existence in community certain constraints upon their lives. In order to be of greatest value, such constraints must claim allegiance in a manner different from the curse. The curse is self-imposed and its effect is understood to work automatically upon the one who does what is prohibited in the self-curse. Nor must the constraints threaten death in a more juridical way. Nor must they be supported and framed by arrangements for the punishment of those who violate a treaty. The prohibitions must have a character different from that of curse ritual or treaty or code of law that contains the specification of punishment to follow upon stated misdeeds. What is needed is a set of prohibitions that cover wide areas of human conduct, sum these up, and laconically state that they are not to be done.

Viewed in this light, the commandment not to take the life of a fellow human being is intended to be as broad as it is put. It affirms more clearly than Gen. 9:6 that human life belongs to God. In Genesis 9 the tradition is attempting to account for the development of life on earth to the then present day by showing that in the beginning human beings ate plants and fruit and herbs but not other animal life. After the flood ended, God graciously arranged for human beings to take the life of animals for food, but excluding the life blood of such animals, since the very life of the animal is concentrated in the blood, according to ancient Semitic belief. Genesis 9:6 then says that in the taking of life human life must not be shed, unless it should be at the express demand of God himself. In this commandment, the exclusive claims of God are being underscored not for the purpose of offering cases to guide the judges and not for the purpose of stating exact penalties to be laid upon violators, and certainly not for the purpose of warning the community, with solemn dread, not to run the risk of falling under the divine curse by doing forbidden deeds. Rather, the exclusive claim of God is stated much more formally and summarily, with a set of prohibitions governing relations between the community and God (commandments one, two, and three), between the community and God as expressed through the basic institutions of the Sabbath and the family (commandments four and five) and between and among the members of the community itself (commandments six, seven, eight, nine, and ten). Two of these latter five govern basic requirements of human beings as such (commandments six and seven), while the remaining three (commandments eight, nine, and ten) deal with basic social obligations of humankind. Such a division of the commandments could of course have occurred without prior reflection. It would still not be right to call it an accidental grouping, for there is often at work in such matters an interior logic that a community or an individual might well not recognize.

We have, then, a commandment designed to protect without qualification the life of human beings from acts of violence threatening the continued existence of life itself. This prohibition leads the list. Its basic assertion or background is the recognition that life belongs to God and to God alone. A commandment not to kill, then, must depend upon the earlier list of commandments, where the claim of God over the whole of life and the demand to acknowledge that claim through unqualified allegiance to God are stated. First came the commandments that assure that the community and its individual members will take as the central reality of life the presence and power of God. They will have no rival deities to dilute their commitment to the one God. They will not act to control the power of this one God, nor will they use that power to do damage to others. One day in seven will be set apart from the rest as a sign that Israel has made such a commitment to Yahweh and will honor that commitment. No normal labors will occur on that seventh day, both because God will have rest from labor as well as work, and because human beings and draft animals also require rest from grinding toil. Instead of elaborate rites to assure that the dead do not return and do damage on this earth to the living, the ancient Israelites devoted themselves to the life and care of the living. This care continued to the very moment of death, even when the parents or grandparents had grown old and were no longer able to care for themselves. Israel had no need to continue to reverence the dead ancestors;[3] she did need to see to it that the bond connecting the generations was maintained, neither being thrown aside when the parents were no longer of economic value to the community nor keeping the living generation bound in unwholesome ways to the generation of those that had died.

In that context the commandment not to take human life is set. As noted above, the commandment was probably never understood by the ancient Israelites to rule out in principle the taking of the life of the murderer or the exorcist or the blasphemer or the others who did deeds of such violence or horror that the community could not endure letting the perpetrator live. Nor did the commandment rule out acts of warfare. But this commandment nevertheless was centrally important in shaping the mentality and the ethos of Israelite understandings of acts of violence against fellow human beings. No such act could be done, not when the Ten Commandments were functioning within the society properly, without reference to the basic datum that life belongs exclusively to God. Once again we see how the Decalogue probably functioned in the life of ancient Israel, driving home the recognition by young and old alike that the kinds of acts not to be done under any circumstances would even so now and again have to be done. How could these acts be done? How could murderers be put to death, given the understanding that life belonged to God exclusively? The answer would have been that God knows the need to take the life of this murderer and accepts such a violation as appropriate, for the murderer if not killed will simply take other life and thus himself violate the commandment again and involve us in his guilt, since we could have prevented his doing additional acts of murder by taking his life.

The point is, however, that routinely and from earliest youth the community of Israel would have been warned by its recitation of this sixth commandment that such a taking of human life was not to be routine, was not to become simply a part of the ordinary practice of administering justice. The taking of human life in warfare would normally require a decision on Yahweh's part that the war was called for, although it does seem likely that engagement in war did in fact become quite routine. The taking of human life as punishment for the crime of murder was done under the strict requirement that there be eyewitnesses and that the testimony of these witnesses be in agreement. Acts of killing that were judged inadvertent or justified by the situation required a decision by the community or its appointed judges that such was in fact the case. More and more in the later history of Israel the commandment was safeguarded by clarification of the tests that must be met before the community could apply the death penalty to any perpetrator of a crime considered to be a capital crime.

The commandment not to take human life may also have been casting its influence over other aspects of life in the course of Israel's history. By the time of Jesus the commandment not to kill had probably already colored the community's attitude toward acts of violence of any sort. This it was intended to do from the start. Even so, for us the commandment not to take human life has assumed ramifications far beyond any likely to have been dreamed of in ancient times. We know how to prevent conception and thus can see to it that certain potential lives not appear on the earth. Has this commandment anything to do with control and regularization of birth? We know how, with little apparent damage to the mother, to remove an embryo from the womb so that the life (or potential life) will in fact not appear at the normal time but be laid aside. Has this commandment anything to do with abortion? We know how seemingly unbearable life can become, how pointless, how unnecessary, as in some cases of terminal illness or related disabilities such that life, by most standard definitions, is already curtailed almost to the point of having ceased. Is euthanasia to be considered when we deal with the sixth commandment?

In my judgment, all these matters do relate to the intention of the sixth commandment, especially as that commandment is developed through the centuries in Judaism and in Christianity. One reminder may be necessary, however. There was in ancient Israel no notion of the sanctity of human life in and of itself. The sanctity of human life lies in the action and the will of Yahweh as these are revealed to the people of Israel. God himself protects human life, and Israel is required to follow the path of God in protecting human life. Human life has its basic meaning in relation to God's own purpose for life and not in the sheer fact of life itself. Such an understanding makes it unlikely that ancient Israel would have had the difficulty we have with the matter of capital punishment. When a person stands guilty under the specified requirements of the covenant law, that person can be executed if the witnesses agree. If Yahweh commands that an act of warfare be engaged in, then the people need feel no compunction in carrying out that kind of action, even though it may result in the death of many. No abstract statement about the sanctity of human life can be derived from the sixth commandment. Life belongs to God—that is an understanding different from the view that life is in itself sacrosanct.

Once that point has been granted, however, we find ourselves still with our list of possible areas of application of this commandment. If life belongs to God, human beings are not free to take a life without thought of its having been given to the particular person by God himself. How do I dare infringe upon the prerogatives of the Author and Giver of all life? More particularly, how do I act in such a way as to impose my will upon a situation that is governed by God alone?

God has called his people Israel into existence, has given to them their particular allotment of land in the world, and has promised them that a great future awaits them. He has warned of the consequences of their turning their backs upon him and spurning his commandments. But God has indicated that there is a life to be lived by the individual members of the community of Israel and that the community's health is affected by the actions of each member. Therefore, when I dare to take the life of a fellow Israelite, I am challenging Yahweh's gift of life and of a place in Israel for that individual. Similarly with the personal and property goods of that person, as we shall see below, God shows his goodness to us in providing land and goods and possibilities of life; to act against these gifts of God to another person is quite different from some violation of an abstract "right of property." This laconic commandment not to kill, then, has behind it the gift of life from God, first of all to the people Israel as their special reception of life and a future from Yahweh, but also as a gift of life to every human being. The import of the statement in Gen. 9:6 is evident, for the prohibition of taking human life is underscored by the declaration that God made humankind in his own image.

Yet we can see from the generalization found in this priestly addition to the old legal couplet ("God made human beings in his own image") that the commandment not to kill does have applicability well beyond the range of Israel's geographic boundaries. No one within Israel dares to take such an action against one whom God has called into being and for whom God has a special place and purpose in the world, not if any alternative exists. But neither shall anyone take such action against a fellow human being without the most solemn recollection that this life is itself the gift of a good God. If the community is in a position to claim that it is taking human life in obedience to this commandment rather than in defiance of it, well and good. Such application of the commandment has been claimed through the centuries and perhaps with full justification. The murderer who already has killed must be stopped before he proceeds with his obvious intention of taking yet another life. If the death of the murderer is the only way of restraining him and thus preventing a second murder, the murderer's death is in fact required, it would seem, by the commandment not to take human life. For if I am able to stop the second act of murder and do not do so, I am certainly a part of that act of murder.

Even so, many efforts have been made through the centuries to calculate the relative harm done by such readiness to engage in acts of violence in order to prevent further violence by others. How well we know the abuses to which such a line of thinking has been subjected! And the circle of violence has continued through the centuries. Persons rarely seem content to respond to acts of violence with just the requisite amount of violence to prevent further damage by the initial perpetrator. Rather, they go further than necessary and are apparently conditioned by such engagement in violence to resort to violence all the more quickly on a second occasion. For this reason, it has been argued, some person or some group or some generation of human beings must be ready to try, at whatever cost to themselves, their group, or their generation, to break this circle of violence. On this premise, the commandment not to kill must be adhered to scrupulously. Persons doing violence against fellow human beings may be restrained, but their lives may not be taken. Groups and nations may suffer desperate harm at the hands of evildoers, but they dare not resort to acts of killing in order to put a stop to the killings perpetrated by others. Better to suffer the loss of life than to allow the vicious circle of bloodshed to continue year after year and century after century.

In principle there is no reason why our commandment might not have had this sweeping import implicit within it. There is no doubt that the commandment, as applied by Israel's great prophets, served to illuminate all sorts of acts of violence, all kinds of brutalization of personal and social life. In Hosea's use of the latter part of the Decalogue, for example, all the violations of the commandments add up to the dreadful picture of "blood following upon blood," bloodshed rife within the land, with no one caring, no one heeding, not even the appointed leaders (Hos. 4:2). Nor is there any doubt whatever that the promised time of consummation, when God's purposes on a transformed earth begin to be realized, would be marked by an end of such violence. The bloodstained garments and the blood-flecked boots of the warriors would become no more than fuel for the fire (Isa. 9:5; Hebrew, 9:4). No longer would there be any hurting, any destroying, at the holy mountain of Zion. And what obtained at the holy center would spread out to encompass the entire earth (Isa. 11:9).[4]

The prophets were nourished on the laws of the covenant and on their demand for authentic righteousness, care for the life of fellow human being, commitment to peace and wholeness of life. Their nourishment in all probability owed a great deal to the repeated quotation of the sixth commandment in its stark simplicity: "Thou shalt not kill."

Even though we conclude, as I do, that the sixth commandment does not require a pacifist rigor for its application to count, the import of such a commandment for the common life today is both devastating and glorious. It stakes out the claim of Yahweh upon all human life, insisting not upon the sanctity of life in some general or abstract sense but on the exclusiveness of God's ownership of life. All human life, with other forms of life also drawn in along the way, is tied to its Creator and Sustainer and Consummator in such a way that it is simply not the prerogative of any human being to dispose of such life except as the human being, or the community, can claim to be acting directly on behalf of God in doing so. In this way alone can the human community lay aside the thoroughgoing pacifist implication of the commandment. Human life cannot be taken—not even by means of capital punishment administered by the most just and thoroughgoing system of justice conceivable—unless it is done on behalf of God. But that rules out capital punishment entirely, in a day when no society would wish, presumably, to act directly on God's behalf. And for the protection of other life capital punishment need not be adopted. It is, of course, the surest way to see that a murderer will not murder again. But in an imperfect world it will also inevitably mean occasionally the execution of the innocent. And sentences to life imprisonment that really keep the incorrigible in prison for life and unable any longer to destroy life are more appropriate acts of the community against murderers and others who cannot or will not refrain from destroying the lives of others. That some murderers might prefer death to life imprisonment is of no consequence whatever to the community that wishes to keep from falling victim to the blood-lust that seems always close at hand when the death penalty is regularly resorted to in cases of capital crimes.

What of the other aspects of the taking of human life? Karl Barth has shown how this commandment enables the community to test its actions that result in the loss of human life, or in life's being snuffed out as it appears, or in its not being permitted to begin.[5] In all such instances it is of immense help to keep this short and unqualified commandment in view. When abortions are available on request and there is no need even to give thought to the matter of a mysterious gift of life, present as a result of the action of two persons, then the commandment not to kill is not functioning well in the society. It functions well, at least minimally well, when it helps the partners involved in the conception and bearing of a child-to-be reflect on what they have done, what the alternatives facing them at that time are, and where among such alternatives lies the course of action best able to fulfill the claim of life and the mystery of life being exercised upon and within them.

Similarly, the taking of one's own life by a person who apparently has lost all possibility of continuing in life meaningfully is challenged by this commandment. Does the person contemplating suicide as the acceptable way of dealing with terminal illness find that he or she is in a position to claim the prerogatives of God and act on God's behalf? It may well be so, but if it is so, then time is needed for reflection, and the family and the community probably should not be ignored and the decision not be taken in isolation. And if the issue is whether to withhold special means of keeping a person alive when that person's prospect for recovery or for any sort of meaningful existence is virtually eliminated, then there, too, the people most closely involved need to be ready to face the same question: Is the withholding of such medical or technical treatment something that conforms to the fundamental principle that life belongs to God and to God alone?

Regarding warfare, the situation seems quite different. Here, as in the case of the restraint of evildoers generally by violence that may issue in their death, one has to calculate relative values and be willing to be guided, among other things, by an ethical norm that considers the greatest good of the greatest number. In principle it can be concluded that just wars do not exist and probably never did exist. Wars have been waged in which the issues were relatively clear, as in the case of the resistance against Nazism by those who, much too late, were moved to counteract a monstrous evil that had already been applied to the extermination of an entire people. But wars ought by definition to be understood to be the result of massive evil taking possession of peoples and nations. Never would a matter come to warfare without there having been more than modest numbers and kinds of misdeeds within the lives of those involved, and among them. Even so, wars will come, for human beings will perpetrate evil against others in such a way that it will be found to be unbearable. When warfare comes, the commandment does not lose its force or power to guide. In acts of warfare, which are wrong and abhorrent, human beings and groups of human beings can be guided by this commandment that insists that life belongs to God and can be taken only by those who are bold enough to act in God's stead. The kinds of warfare chosen are not unimportant. Cluster bombs that kill indiscriminately are worse than other kinds of bombs, though all bombs are horrible instruments of death directed against life that God has given. Bacterial warfare is worse than warfare waged by guns and artillery. Acts of war that show any kind of restraint in the taking of life given by God are better than other acts of war that do not show such restraint. And acts of warfare that arise when at least some of the parties involved have sought to avoid war, have sought to meet the legitimate grievances of the parties claiming to be aggrieved, and have exercised restraint in the waging of war are human activities that are less blatantly a violation of the sixth commandment than if such efforts had not taken place.

In short, the sixth commandment stakes out the claim of God over all life and serves notice to all human beings—but especially to those who claim the biblical heritage as binding upon them—that God's claim upon life is to be given priority in the decisions taken by a community or its individual members.

But how in a secular world can a society act to take seriously the claims of God? What God? What understanding of God is to obtain? We all know the importance of such questions and the difficulty of finding an acceptable answer. We do not need, for example, to speak of the claims of the God of Israel or of Christianity in just the terms found in the biblical literature or in Jewish or Christian theology. In a later chapter we will try to propose what language might be used instead of the "God-talk" of the Bible. Here let it suffice to say that we can insist that the fundamental mystery of life itself needs to be respected as societies and individuals deal with the gift of life and the various ways by which life is also taken. I propose these simple guidelines: (1) Life is a gift, a gift to be treasured. (2) The gift is best treasured as it is shared in association with the lives of others. (3) The forms of association, therefore, that are to be preferred over others are those that enhance rather than damage life in community. (4) Any action that damages or destroys life in community must be rejected, unless that action is only temporarily damaging to life in community and is undertaken in order to assure the continuance of such life in community once the threats against it are removed.

THE SEVENTH COMMANDMENT:
NO CONTEMPT FOR SEX
"THOU SHALT NOT COMMIT ADULTERY WITH THE
WIFE OF THY NEIGHBOR"

Our reconstruction of the seventh commandment adds the *object* of the act of adultery, but since this object is clearly implied the addition does not change the meaning of the commandment but only makes its import explicit. The ancient Near East and the early Israelites recognized that women stood in a protected relationship within the society and thus did not have the freedom that male protectors were given. In ancient Mesopotamian societies at different historical periods women had much larger scope for the exercise of their abilities than, during most epochs, they enjoyed in Israel. But never in the ancient world were women permitted to claim and to enjoy the sexual freedom that men exercised.

This situation is mirrored with regard to adultery. An engaged or married woman committed adultery if she had sexual relations with anyone other than her husband or her betrothed husband-to-be. The man committed adultery only if he had relations with the wife or the betrothed of another man. Thus a man who visited a prostitute would not be committing adultery. Should the woman challenge him, however, and hold him to some promise that he made, as in the case of Tamar and her father-in-law Judah (see Genesis 38), then the visit to the prostitute might take on quite a different character. As for the apostle Paul, he apparently considered that sexual relations with a prostitute constituted a kind of marriage, no matter what the partners intended (see 1 Cor. 6:15–20).[6]

The prohibition against adultery takes the place of a long list of sexual offenses found in the curse ritual of Deuteronomy 27 and in other lists. It is noteworthy that the act of adultery does not appear in two of those lists, the one just mentioned and the Covenant Code. We find in some texts of a later time specifications about rape or the exercise of violence against a woman for sexual purposes (see Deut. 22:25–29), where we also have laws concerning adultery (Deut. 22:22–24). But in the Covenant Code (Exodus 21–23) we have only the law concerning sexual relations with virgins who are not betrothed (22:16–17). In the Holiness Code (Leviticus 18–23) we have such a prohibition at the end of a long list of disallowed sexual relations within the family, where we are told, "You shall not lie carnally with your neighbor's wife, and defile yourself with her" (18:20). Again the prohibition appears in Lev. 20:10, this time at the beginning of a list of sexual offenses within the family. We also have in this collection the distinction drawn between the slave woman, betrothed to another man, and the free woman. Sexual relations with the former do not result in the death penalty for either (Lev. 19:20–22).

Once again, as in the case of the law against killing, we have a very generally stated prohibition, with no definition given and no distinctions drawn. It is the kind of statement that clearly will in times to come encourage an application broader than it probably had in view, just as was the case with the sixth commandment. The distinction between the meaning of adultery for the man and for the woman can easily disappear, as it should. But for ancient Israel the distinction will remain, because the woman is understood to depend in many ways upon the life, protection, and honor of her husband. Adultery for her is any sexual act after betrothal or marriage between her and any male other than her husband. Other sexual acts, such as homosexuality or bestiality, are condemned equally, whether committed by man or by woman.

It is important not to overlook the fact that for ancient Israel there was no prudishness about sex and no notion whatever that while sexual relations were necessary for human reproduction the act was at best morally ambiguous. That view came from other, later societies in which there was a distinction between material and earthly realities and those that transcended all temporal and material representations of them. For some elements in early Greek society, such a view was central. Sexual relations between men, for example, were thought to be on a much higher and more intellectual-spiritual level than those between man and woman. And in later mystic-religious communities an actual contempt for physical sexual relations developed and was taught. Such views, as is well known, were widely held in the early Christian centuries in many parts of the Mediterranean world and did great mischief within the Christian church.

This commandment against adultery does not in any way aim at such a development. It is apparently intended to protect the life and selfhood of the married or betrothed woman; it also aims at the preservation of the institution of marriage. Some interpreters have overstressed the idea of the woman as property of the man in ancient Israel and have maintained that this commandment and others in the list give too much space to the protection of property in Israel. Actually, the laws of Israel do involve, as we shall see later, strong emphasis upon the right of families and individuals to have personal possessions and to be able to keep these as one's own. But Israel gives much less prominence to property than it does to human beings and their rights, in contrast to the more highly developed societies in Mesopotamia and in Egypt, as we can see from the legal collections of the ancient world that have come to light thus far.

It is important to have the setting in view as we try to get to the central meaning of this commandment. Not only is there no denigration of sex between man and woman in ancient Israel, but there is positive commitment to the place of sexual relations and there is enjoyment of sex. It has often been maintained that in ancient Israel sexual relations are understood to be for the purpose of procreation only and never for mere enjoyment. Certainly, the command to fill the earth and subdue it in Gen. 1:28 stresses the anticipated fruit of the union of man and woman, while passages that condemn onanism, if taken to be against any form of sexual relations that avoids the normal possibility of the woman's conceiving a child, would seem also to underscore the unique meaning of sex as for the bearing of children (see Gen. 38:8–10). But the sin of Onan was his failure to provide offspring for his dead brother and thus continue the brother's name in Israel, not the way in which he did so. And such passages as Gen. 18:12 show us a quite unreflective identification of sexual relations with one's partner as a matter of "having fun." It is possible, of course, that Sarah in that passage is thought of as having the pleasure of bearing a child, but that would not be the most natural and obvious meaning of the text. See also Prov. 5:15–20.

The prohibition against adultery stakes out the claim of the two partners in marriage to a relationship between themselves that is not to be compromised or destroyed by the action of either partner. While the law does allow for the man to marry more than one wife, it specifies limits to his favoring the one over the other. One ancient piece of legislation requires the man not to diminish sexual relations between himself and a slave-wife or concubine; if he does so, she secures her freedom for that reason alone (see Exod. 21:10). In ancient Israel, the man is given latitude beyond that available to the woman in sexual matters but the law does not do more than tacitly admit that such is the case; there is no theological justification for that situation. And the act of having sexual relations, as noted above, is understood to carry with it a sharing of life in such depth that it creates unity between the sexual partners. In this respect we have one of the most interesting and important developments in sexual understanding found in the entire ancient Near Eastern world.

There is ample evidence that the ancient world knew the mystery of sexual relations and was deeply affected by that mystery. The sharing of life sexually, and the participation in an act of creation in which human life was brought forth from the body of the woman after sexual sharing between her and the male partner, represented for ancient folk an unmistakable analogy to the mystery of creation itself. And for ancient folk creation was not something that occurred once long ago; it was a central reality for everyday life, one of the mysteries attested every day that one lived. The ancient societies understood themselves to be related to the realm of the gods through sexual activity in a particularly intimate and critical way. The bringing of fertility to earth itself came about through the sacred marriage of the gods, one issue of which was such fruitfulness on earth. Animal life, some plant life, and the life of human beings in particular were all, in their sharing the process of creation and renewal of life on the earth, an earthly counterpart to archetypal activities centered within the realm of the gods in the heavens.[7]

Sexual activity, then, for most ancient folk was one of the most unmistakable indicators of the transcendence of ordinary historical existence by those who, sexually, could intimately be caught up into the realm of the gods, share in the re-creation of earth, and imitate cultically the very power and being of the high gods. For ancient folk sexual relations were earthy, and also fun; but for most of the ancient Near Eastern peoples they were in the realm of sacrament as well.

In ancient Israel this understanding of sex and of sexuality, especially human sexuality, changed drastically, for reasons difficult to trace. The mystery of sexual relations certainly was not lost or denied; it was deeply known and felt. But sex was removed from the mystical realm, as were other human activities, to the extent at least that sexual relations were understood not as an act of participation in the process by which the gods renewed life on earth but as an act by which creatures of God carried on, as creatures, a relationship between themselves that was regulated by God's purposes for them on this earth.

The sexual taboos of most societies are explained by reference to myths and stories of their origins that show the fateful consequences of overstepping the sexual boundaries (relations within the family declared to be too close, or the like). It seems likely that many of Israel's sexual taboos arose in the situation of conflict between Israelite religious understandings and practices and those of the Canaanite neighbors. The horror with which homosexuality or bestiality or too close sexual relations within the family are viewed in Israel lends support to this idea. While sexual customs in a society are shaped by forces that are often impossible to trace back to their origins, it seems almost certain that the lawgivers of ancient Israel are much more concerned about the religious danger of some of the sexual practices prohibited than they are about the actual character of the sexual acts themselves. No doubt homosexuality was also understood as a failure to take up the commandment to be fruitful, multiply, and fill the earth if the homosexual did not marry and have a family or attempt to do so. And the sexual activities that characterized worship at some of the shrines in early Israel were condemned because they were, from the viewpoint of Israel's prophets, orgies and instances of a luxury and wastefulness of time, energy, and goods that would not please Yahweh. But, more important, I believe, the attacks of Hosea and others upon the sexual practices associated with the cult were attacks upon a people who were mixing two religious understandings and the practices appropriate to each. This the prophets would not endure.

This commandment is extremely terse and short, leaving aside many of the matters in the sexual realm that must have confronted the judges and lawgivers every day. It is a simple prohibition of the act of adultery, with no reference whatever to any of the other sexual offenses, with no reference to the institution of prostitution, with no harking back to the life of the first man and the first woman in the garden, with no specification as to what the institution of polygamy might have to do with adultery, and with not a word said about the punishment that was to befall the adulterer or the adulteress. As in the case of killing, the law against adultery simply states the prohibition and does so in an unqualified way.

It is this laconic form of the prohibition that makes the commandment so powerful. It implies an understanding of the relation between husband and wife, or two betrothed persons, as a relation that is not to be terminated short of death unless the very gravest of situations require its termination. It is, by the act itself, a sealing and cementing of the life of each to the life of the other. It rules out the notion of casual sexual relations, not by implying some metaphysical character to sexual relations but by implying that (as Gen. 2:18–25 indicates in its myth of the first human pair in the Garden) sexual engagement reunites male and female in an entity of humankind such that the union so created is not transferable from partner to partner without grievous harm to each partner in the union. For the ancient Israelite, or for leaders within the community of ancient Israel responsible for this understanding of the sixth commandment, sex is good, sex is fun, sex is a sharing of life between partners that does not draw those partners into some mystic realm of divine creativity such that they are thereby identified with the divine Creator-pair from whom sexual creativity derives. It does, however, call into existence here on earth a new unity, a joining of one man and one woman in a sexual life together such that a new entity has been created, the nucleus of the family, the entity that requires a male human being to leave the confines of his own family, his father and his mother, and cling to his wife in a way comparable to that in which he once was tied to his parents. His life is now completed in her life, and his life, as completed in hers, is complicated and endangered only if his relations should involve the wife of another male human being who also has left father and mother to cling to his wife, becoming one flesh with her.

For the author of Genesis 2 monogamous marriage is certainly the norm in view. Marriage of more than one wife may have been fairly common in ancient Israel; it never was ruled out in principle. But we can see from this commandment against adultery and from other sexual guidelines in the Hebrew Bible that polygamy always brought or threatened complications. One was not to have sexual relations with the wife of another man, and a woman was to have sexual relations only with her betrothed or husband. Any other kind of arrangement would destroy life in community, the ancient Israelites believed.

We know, of course, that adultery occurred. Specific legislation is developed because adultery occurred. Stories of acts of adultery are frequent in the Old Testament. And many acts of adultery doubtless occurred in ancient Israel without the knowledge of the partner in marriage or of the community. Acts of adultery do not destroy marriages, not always and perhaps not even very often. The Israelite ideology concerning sexual relations between a married person and someone else may therefore be questioned on empirical grounds as well as on the basis of changing understandings of what marriage is and ought to be considered to be. Indeed, it might be possible to say that this commandment, perhaps more than any other in the list, must be set aside today, as persons have learned a new joy and fulfillment in life through the adoption of much freer relations between human beings sexually. Many a person today—indeed, many a Christian theologian today—will wish to urge upon the Christian community that it never again get trapped into espousing a notion of what is permitted sexually that does terrible damage to individuals and to families and to the larger human community.

Finally, it could be claimed, the society has begun to throw off its bondedness to outmoded and crippling understandings of human sexuality, often passed along to the new generation by means of religious teaching. Finally, it is said, human beings are beginning to be able to realize that so long as physical harm to the sexual partner is avoided and so long as no party is exploited by the other, persons can and should find sexual enjoyment in whatever way "works" for them. Marriage may itself be a somewhat outmoded institution today, given the encrusted traditions concerning divorce, relations between divorced couples and their children, and disposal of property in the event of divorce. The commandment against adultery might be restated, at the most, to underscore commitment and to support partners in committing themselves to one another sexually in such a way as actually to reflect the commitment they are making to each other as a whole. The chief thing is that human beings continue to commit themselves to one another honestly, truthfully, and lovingly, avoiding deception, exploitation, and irresponsible conduct of any kind. The two partners may by open decision agree that sexual relations with others are acceptable, perhaps within agreed-upon bounds. Why not? It appears that many marriages have been saved by the discovery, often with professional help, of just what is lacking sexually within that marriage and by a process of discovering, with the help of sexual partners other than the marriage partner, what is possible sexually that is enriching and fulfilling.

And sexual experience prior to marriage seems to be more and more common on the part of men and women. Is there some magic in the marriage act that makes such experience after marriage, perhaps only occasionally, so threatening to the marriage?

As in the case of killing, it cannot be claimed that this commandment should become an absolutistic and unbreakable norm, issuing in a commitment never to have sexual relations with anyone other than the marriage partner. But unlike the sixth commandment, this seventh commandment does allow for scrupulous adherence without any necessary harm at all. It is difficult to find a situation comparable to that of the pacifist who will not, because he or she cannot, lift a finger to restrain the taker of other life.

It therefore seems entirely in order for us to claim that this prohibition can be the guideline for every marriage, expressing the commitment of the partners in marriage to treasure and preserve a unity that has been called into being in marriage and in the sexual relations they have engaged in as marriage partners. And certainly it would seem evident that, if sexual relations do in fact relate persons to one another in ways deeper than might then and there be realized, the wise course is for married persons to have sexual relations with no one other than their spouse, ever.

The commandment may also have implications beyond the marriage relationship. What of sexual relations before marriage, or in no relation to any plan for marriage? What of prostitution? What of homosexual relations? Of relations with animals? Of masturbation? In my view, the chief implications of this commandment for human sexual activity as such are two. First, sexual relations according to biblical religion express a giving of life and love and a receiving of life and love that make any kinds of sexual activity for which that giving and receiving is minimized not only unwise but at least moderately dangerous. Sexual activity by its nature aims at the sharing of life and love with the partner. There are no doubt levels of such giving of life and love, and there is certainly nothing wrong in the pleasure derived by the individual to which that individual may also have contributed. One acid test is evident: Is the relationship one in which I find benefits and pleasure at the expense of someone else? Exploitation of human beings is wrong and inadmissible.

Second, one may ask whether the sexual activity commends and enhances life or whether it damages or threatens to damage life. In this connection, empirical evidence is the very best kind to be guided by. It seems evident that masturbation does not in fact do to those who give pleasure to themselves in this way the things that it was once thought to do. That should settle the matter, although it needs to be borne in mind how the community can share this kind of information so that the continuation of taboos and misinformation no longer do the damage done in the past. It also seems evident that homosexual activity does not always constitute or lead to irresponsible sexual activity or to the damaging or destroying of individual, group, or public morals. The dangers of exploitative sex do seem to be higher in the realm of homosexual relations, but it is not certain that they need to be higher.

In sexual relations outside marriage it is often thought that persons learn to give and receive life and love in ways that enhance the life of both partners, and that this is one of the most positive aspects of the sexual revolution of contemporary times. I wonder if the statement does not need some qualification. There is no reason to deny that sometimes there are such commitments to the life of the partner and such love shared that the sexual partnership is, so far as one can see, quite unexceptionable. But think of the numerous instances in which even when there is no exploitation there is less than an enhancement of life. Sexual relations often precede any kind of commitment to one another on other levels, and if the sexual act itself brings a bond, through its being engaged in, is that bond not likely to do harm when not followed by the other commitments? In short, is casual or moderately committed sexual activity really possible without damage? I am not sure that it is. Think of the prostitutes who have come to detest the persons of the opposite sex with whom this commercial transaction is carried out. Some may escape its damaging virus, but apparently most do not. Think of the many instances in which young men do in fact damage sexual partners even though they have no such thing in mind. Think of the marriages that have been made the more difficult by sexual relations prior to marriage that set the level of sexual expectation for one or both married partners.

But basically, the commandment against adultery simply embodies enormous wisdom and power and needs therefore no defense today. If the relations between the generations, parents and children, are being addressed in the fifth commandment, the relations between husband and wife, between two persons betrothed to one another, are regulated here. Damaging the former relationship can be ruinous for the life of the newer generation. Damaging of the latter relationship can be even more devastating to the current generation and to the coming one. Sexual relations suffice between one man and one woman. Who can deny that? Why, then, should we not give our allegiance to this wise guideline and let it be the norm even if now and again transgressed? Surely, no one any longer can seriously challenge the view that sexual faithfulness in marriage is good.[8]

CHAPTER 6

Basic Social Obligations

THE EIGHTH COMMANDMENT: NO CONTEMPT
FOR THE GOODS OF THE COMMUNITY
"THOU SHALT NOT STEAL ANYTHING
THAT IS THY NEIGHBOR'S"

The remaining three commandments refer to regulation of life in community in such a fashion as to assure that human beings and families can maintain their place and their rights within it. In ancient Israel there was no notion of the inviolability of things owned by individuals or families. The development of the "right to property" and to its exclusive ownership and use is a part of the Western world. Even so, the ancient Israelites did recognize, as did their neighbors, that goods were an extension of the life of the family and that the rights of communities, families, and individuals necessarily involved their right to maintain those goods —goods that were in fact such an extension of the "self" of the individual or family or community.

Each of these three commandments, however, is quite distinct. Commandment eight, in our view, could in fact be left as the tradition has preserved it—as a direct and general prohibition of theft. Scholars have proposed in recent years that it refers to the stealing of a human being rather than to the goods of an individual,[1] but that specific interpretation, widely accepted these days, seems unlikely. Rather, the commandment prohibits any interference by others in the family and its goods. The commandment not to steal simply means not to claim for one's own the possessions of another. We have nonetheless seen fit to lengthen the commandment slightly to include the object: "anything that is thy neighbor's."

Commandment nine is concerned with the maintenance of a structure of public administration indispensable to the preservation of life in community and to the regulation of how the goods of the family or individual are to be secured. Testimony given before the judges or in public administration is not to be false testimony. Just as one must not take for oneself what belongs to another, so one is not to make, before the community, assertions or claims that do not correspond to reality.

Commandment ten has in view a hankering after the goods of others or the life of others, and doing so in such a way as to be drawn by lust or unwholesome desire into making plans to take these as one's own. It is different from the eighth commandment in that it does refer (contrary to the judgment of several recent interpreters) to the unnatural desire for these goods of others, not simply to the making of plans to take these goods for one's own.[2]

All three of these commandments, then, deal with basic social obligations: the obligation to leave one's fellow Israelite in possession of his or her goods; the obligation to speak the truth in public testimony before the authorities and thus to make it possible for the community's institutions to function; and the obligation to refrain from overweening desire for the items that make up the household of one's neighbor, be these the neighbor's wife or draft animals or the livestock maintained to make a living, or any goods belonging to the neighbor.

The first of these, the command against stealing, has been badly misused in the course of Western history. Persons have been able, frequently by unjust means, to accumulate for themselves such a quantity of the goods of the earth that they have as a result been almost invincible in any plans that they saw fit to make. The accumulation of wealth means the accumulation of power. Often the victims of the rich have been desperately mistreated when they dared to take even the smallest amount of the property of the wealthy, a theme widely treated in the literatures

of the Western world. For the Israelite community, at least theo-
retically, several constraints worked to prevent this kind of drastically unequal distribution of the goods of the earth that Yahweh
provided. The community was required by the covenant law not
to deal violently with the weak and the poor and those left without normal supports of family life. They were to remember that
they—each individual Israelite—were all descendants of slaves
in Egypt, persons oppressed by those more wealthy and powerful
than they. They were never to forget this fact. They should know
the heart of the oppressed, the stranger, the poor, the victimized;
how could they then become victimizers, oppressors, hostile to
the stranger in their midst? To do so would be to impose on
others the very conditions of life in which their God once found
them and from which, out of his mercy, he delivered them.

Concrete legislation provided for the life of the poor and the
weak. When the grain was harvested, some was to be left for the
poor. Persons were permitted to eat their fill as they passed
through the property of the neighbor, but they were not to gather
fruit or the like to take home. And the institution of the Jubilee
Year, whether or not actually put in effect at any time within the
concrete history of ancient Israel, certainly spoke against unnatural accumulations of personal property. In theory, each male
Israelite was to have his part of the patrimony of Yahweh in the
Promised Land. If such a holding were lost because of tragedy or
even neglect, once in fifty years the holdings were to return to
their original owner, so that all families would have their personal
stake in the promised goods of the earth from Yahweh.

The prophets never ceased to inveigh against those who were
land-hungry and who took advantage of the poor and the weak,
amassing for themselves wealth beyond any imaginable need.
Those who "joined house to house and field to field" were perverting the very purpose of God in bringing his people into a
rich and goodly land (Isa. 5:8). Israelites were clearly warned to
respect the right of the neighbor to possess goods that extended
and enriched his or her life. But there was not by any means an
unbridled commitment to the "right of property" in the sense
that such a right was later to develop.

Our commandment, as noted above, has been thought to refer to one particular kind of private capital. It is often said that the closest equivalent to the "original" eighth commandment is found in Exod. 21:16: "Whoever steals a man, whether he sells him or is found in possession of him, shall be put to death."[3] The commandment, in this view, should read, "Thou shalt not steal any man from thy neighbor." Otherwise, so it is said, the eighth and the tenth commandments are much too similar, since the verb translated "to covet" means not simply to lust after but to take effective action to secure—that is, to steal!

Such an interpretation is forced and implausible. As we shall see in dealing with the tenth commandment, the verb does mean "to covet," "to have it in mind to do a certain thing," and not necessarily the carrying through of that determination. And here it is quite implausible that a commandment is directed against the presumably very occasional practice of stealing and making one's own property the slave belonging to one's neighbor. In the small acreage that constituted the life-world of most ancient Israelites, there would not have been any way to hide from the owner the slave taken into one's possession. And the commandment to avoid coveting the property of one's neighbor is itself not sufficiently direct in outlawing theft of the goods of one's neighbor. Theft is always a problem for any community. In ancient Israel the eighth commandment quite simply rules it out, but it does so in an environment that prevents property from becoming as important as human life, or indeed more important.

Therein lies the continuing import of this commandment for today. Rather than its being used (as often it has in fact been used) to assure wealthy individuals that they may proceed unchecked in the amassing of wealth, confident that the laws will protect their property at whatever cost to the poor or the weak or the desperate, this commandment can be applied precisely against those who amass wealth and accumulate goods by any and all means. When equally applied, the eighth commandment has much more to say to the giver of bribes for political favors, to the manipulator of the economic system for unjust and unearned assets, to the destroyer of businesses for the sake of a favorable

tax advantage, to the issuer of stocks who having made his millions then sells out as the vast new enterprise is about to collapse,
or to the governmental figure who sets out to make a fortune by
compelling the offering of bribes. The stealing with which our
society is more and more familiar lies in such areas as these.

But stealing is stealing, no matter who does it. There might be
the taking of the goods of others in circumstances that make the
act understandable (the raiding in slum areas of businesses
thought to have profited heartlessly at the expense of the poor
residents of the slums, for example), but it would be fatal to
claim that such an act was not only understandable but also justi-
fiable. The most that can be said is that others share responsibility for the act when they have had opportunity to help relieve
the conditions that led to the stealing but have not done so or
have done so inadequately.

In this connection we can see that this commandment against
stealing, located here in the Decalogue, makes it unmistakable
that the Decalogue is *not* by any means Israel's ancient criminal
code. This commandment is not dealing with stealing as equally
serious before the law with murder or adultery. Stealing is not a
capital offense except in the case of the stealing of a human being
(Exod. 21:16), and yet stealing is a kind of action that if not
checked means there can be no life in community whatsoever.
All too often, persons sensitive to the evils that have come from
honoring the right to property have not realized that such a commandment is essential to the checking of rampant capitalism and
unqualified claims to the right to hold property. The ancient legislation of Israel makes it clear that one is not to show partiality
in judgment to any person, not to the rich in defiance of the rights
of the poor and not to the poor in defiance of the rights of others.
The most telling statement of this call to impartial judgment is
found in Lev. 19:15. Indeed, that section of Leviticus 19 is a
marvelous use of the prohibitions of the Decalogue in the manner in which they were intended to be used (see esp. Lev. 19:
1–18).

Should it not be stressed, however, that for us today the commandment against stealing does more harm than good? We do

not think of property as an extension of the self. Rather, we see unmistakably that human realities must take precedence over property. One of the most devastating statements made about the so-called neutron bomb was that it was deadly effective in taking human life but did much less damage to property than conventional bombs or other nuclear weapons. A bomb that protects property while taking human life is the ideal instrument of Western capitalism, it was said! We understand such a response, whether or not it was a sound reaction from the point of view of contemporary world politics.

But has our generation gone beyond the notion of property as the extension of the self and the family? The answer is both yes and no. Regarding some goods that are important to our lives today, there probably should not be any thought at all of their being an important embodiment of our life, our ideas, our commitments. Much of the material on which contemporary Western life depends is simply a convenience, an arrangement of the goods of the earth to serve the interests of people, to relieve the tedium of life, or to ease the expenditure of physical energy. Objects made by machines that are themselves made by machines that have been designed by other machines can have little power to express the life-commitments of human beings.

But it seems likely that no human being and no community should be without objects that are understood as an extension of the life of the community or the individual. One of the great difficulties of our time is that families and individuals have no such attachment to things, things valued as a part of the very life of those who live with the things. Family life loses stability, family play is made more difficult, and the very understanding of the world as God's creation is gravely weakened by such developments. The incredible wastefulness of much of Western life makes matters worse. We replace the furnishings of our homes, and even the homes themselves, to such an extent and with such frequency that we are virtually without personal possessions that count for anything; individuals and families can assemble their households on short notice when they move, there being very little to move with them from one household to another. The loss of goods through theft in such a situation is simply a matter to be reported to the insurance agent. In such situations it is the next commandment, the ninth, that is more likely to come into play: do not bear false testimony to the insurance company's representatives!

The sad thing is that many persons today no longer have treasured household items that continue to maintain the life of the family within and around them. Think of the millions of families around the world that have been uprooted during the last forty years, having lost virtually all they once possessed. Think of what a single item often means to such persons, one memento of the life that has been swept away by warfare or persecution. If the commandment not to steal were related to this situation, and we recognized afresh what it would mean if persons took from us such a treasured possession, then we would be able to understand this commandment better. Ancient societies, and some still surviving today, can understand how essential for life it is to be able to maintain these objects upon which life depends. In ancient Israel the cloak of the poor man was important for survival in the cold nights (see Exod. 22:26 and Amos 2:8).

Indeed, for the very poor, virtually every object possessed was essential for life. For persons of average means, however, loss of property was not a matter of life and death. And yet the commandment not to steal stands right along with those prohibiting murder and adultery. It does so because persons do depend for a wholesome life upon the materials with which that life is surrounded. While it might be a good thing for many of us in the wealthy West to have much of the surfeit of goods we possess stolen from us and never replaced, there are some goods that we unquestionably depend on as the very extension of our lives, our selfhood. Were these to go, it would not be a matter simply of the loss of goods with a "sentimental" value. We would have lost status, substance, qualities that make us who we are.

And it should be so. It should be, indeed, the task of the religious community to help us recover this sort of attachment to the small number of goods that do indeed extend our selfhood outward into other created things. This attachment to things is nothing less than an expression of our commitment to the lives of others and a commitment to the institutions and structures of life that are, in their way, also of fundamental significance for the lives of individuals. When a man and a woman who have lived together for years hold no goods in common—none, that is, that cannot easily and without pain be parted with—then in all likelihood there is little of life given by either to the other that also dare not be parted with. Just as life tended in ancient times to extend outward into the goods upon which life depended, so also those goods were a sign that there was life behind them, a life intended to endure, a life marked by commitments, by love, by a determination to treasure what had been received. Conversely, in our day, when the goods of life held in common have no remaining element of that commitment to one another, when they do not express a life shared, trials endured and surmounted, the joys and the pain of family, then of course such goods are not important, for the life together has not in fact taken root.

The commandment not to steal means, in effect, that persons are not to whittle down, eat away at, the selfhood of individuals or of families or communities. It is a sad thing if the selfhood in individuals and families does not find expression in the goods that fall into their possession. But that implies a relation to the goods that was easier to develop and to sustain in earlier times than today. Perhaps a distinction has to obtain in our lives between those personal goods that do and can body forth our very lives and those that do not and probably cannot or should not. Among the former will certainly be those objects that signal a life shared with others, that call to mind events of significance for us. But such objects might also include those that express the individual's or the family's commitment to care for God's creation, those objects that reflect our own creative response to the created world-order. And that in its turn can mean much for a society once again seeking to discover how to deal responsibly with the limited resources of the planet, how to conserve goods and energy and the natural endowments of the earth. To steal the goods of the current generation is prohibited; is it not also prohibited to steal the goods of the generations yet to appear?

THE NINTH COMMANDMENT: NO CONTEMPT FOR THE COMMUNITY'S INSTITUTIONS "THOU SHALT NOT ANSWER THY NEIGHBOR AS A FALSE WITNESS"

The ninth commandment is concerned with speaking truthfully in public, not about truth-telling in general. There are warnings against lying in ancient legislation and in the Book of Proverbs,[4] and lying is destructive for the liar and often for others. But this commandment has in view the public testimony of individuals before the judges, in social and commercial dealings, and in gatherings for public worship where evildoers were publicly accused and where false accusation could be devastating.

We all know the difference between some really trivial departure from the truth and a serious falsehood. And we need to be aware that some truth-telling is destructive and designed to contribute not to the health of others but to our own mistaken self-esteem. A truthful statement can be a cruel hurt to a fellow human being. The ninth commandment is directed against the serious, destructive perversions of the truth that damage life in community. All institutions of the community are damaged when people do not speak truthfully before fellow members of the community when its affairs are being administered for the good of all.

In ancient Israel, the occasions demanding public truth-telling most frequently were those that regulated public affairs, such as disputes between persons or families over property, other business transactions, or personal injury. When such disputes occurred, the elders or the judges or the heads of households would call for the disputants to make their presentations and bring along their witnesses. The situation is not much different today. The cause of justice can be perverted in many ways: by the guilty person's deliberate refusal to confess the facts and tell the truth; by the accuser's distorting of the facts; by witnesses who lie, either because of a bribe paid them or out of partiality or perverseness; by the judges' or elders' refusal to render fair judgment in face of the evidence presented.

One other situation of grave seriousness was the false accusation of a person in matters where, it was believed, God might bring upon the wrongdoer the punishment of sickness of body or mind. This situation apparently was a very subtle one, often causing persons to believe that someone who was suffering bodily or spiritual disease *must* have done some grave wrong. Since in Israel it was generally believed that sickness did often follow upon sin, as punishment for sin, it was possible for pious and well-meaning persons to accuse the sick one of having done some misdeed. Gossip could be converted into an actual accusation of wrongdoing. In such circumstances the worshiper would need to present himself or herself at the holy place and there make denial of the accusation. God would be expected to serve as the judge of the case, with the priest rendering God's decision.

Our psalms tell of the reactions of worshipers to accusations that people brought or that sick folk believed persons had brought against them. In these situations it seems unlikely that the priests would have called the accusers to appear at the holy place and speak out. But the community did need warning of the consequences of false accusations of persons suffering illness of mind or body. Our commandment provided such warning. One dared not speak, or "answer," falsely in a case at law or in a matter of accusation of sin. The mischievous misuse of God's name to bring the power of the Holy against one's enemy is prohibited by the third commandment. The mischievous misstatement of fact or judgment is prohibited here.

In our own time we have come to see just how imperative it is that human beings speak faithfully and not misleadingly to one another. We also know how difficult it is for many to extricate themselves from the bearing of false witness. Some vocations offer special temptations to the misrepresentation of the truth: advertising of goods for sale; the sale of goods under special pressure to sell at almost any cost to morality; the pressure-laden situations where "success" depends upon bringing persons to act in the desired way, no matter what the means. It is a mistake, however, for anyone to suppose that he or she is free of this temptation. Actually, much of the life we live is tinged by deceptions, shading of the truth, putting ourselves or our proposals in a better light than the facts warrant.

The fabric of society today is so much a product of deception and self-deception that this commandment may appear futile. We may indeed come to distrust virtually all human interchange, believing that at least all our *public* institutions are being manipulated, used for the purpose of misleading and deceiving the populace for the gain of the manipulators. It is hard indeed to deny the corruption of our public institutions today. Corporations bribe public officials on an international and grand scale; government bureaus charged with administering public justice and prosecuting wrongdoers themselves flout public justice; regulatory bodies take bribes from those they are supposed to hold to account; legislators sell their favors to those who are to be constrained from their greed by just and wise legislation; and even heads of governments befoul the institutions of public justice and public administration. Small wonder that cynicism develops and people lose all confidence. One assumes that false testimony is more likely than the true, since speaking falsely wherever necessary serves one's greedy, self-centered, or ideologically fixed ends.

Here, too, as in the case of stealing, it is easy to go too far with one's picture of the corruptness of our common life and its institutions. The speaking of truth in public must apply to all, for the courts must not pervert justice even in favor of the poor. The speaking of the truth may well reveal that the rich and powerful of the earth are sometimes the victims of false testimony too. The poor and the oppressed may break the ninth commandment, but they may, of course, be driven to do so by their desperate need or by deep resentment at the wrongs done them. Public morality is often said to be a matter of concern only to the middle class, and of no interest to the very wealthy and powerful, and a luxury that the poor cannot afford. If so, that only reveals how far from true justice the society has strayed. When a group finds itself the victim of its institutions of public justice, the situation is desperate indeed—like that of the widow whose case was rejected by the unjust judge (see Luke 18:1–8).

However, we must not let truth-telling itself become the occasion for the destruction of the life or the feelings of others. We all know people who are immensely proud of their veracity, their refusal to shade the truth in order to avoid hurting other people. Important as it is to cultivate the practice of speaking the unvarnished truth (see Matt. 5:33–37), it is self-indulgent and supercilious to speak the truth, no matter what harm ensues, merely to protect one's reputation for veracity. One can refuse to lie without always saying the hurtful, damaging, destructive truth. The question of public justice, of the community's larger good, must be kept in clear view. The prophets of Israel never troubled themselves about abstract questions of truth-telling, nor did they argue about whether in any circumstances a white lie might be justified. Their eye was constantly fixed on the issue of public right. Were the courts serving or perverting justice? Were the wealthy taking advantage of the poor? Were judges taking bribes to give favorable decisions? Were people resorting to witchcraft or threatening evil to people if they would not pay the magic-makers? Were prophets—the most dreadful prospect—lying in the name of Yahweh? Any such public resort to falsehood would surely bring ruin to the community.

The ninth commandment issues naturally out of the eighth. Just as one dare not steal the goods of the neighbor by using false weights or measures in the exchange of goods, so one dare not use false words in public transactions. The false word perverts justice as surely as the false weight does. And words do so even more subtly, more perniciously, than false measures or weights. When people twist language to serve their own ends they pollute the very spring of human social existence. Language is the very basis of culture, of human community. When language can no longer be trusted, when words do not express their normal currency but are used for the purpose of deception, the whole community is in gravest danger. That is why Plato attacked the Sophists of his day so mercilessly. That is why a propagandistic or chauvinist or ideologically controlled press is such a danger to all a society's institutions.

It is also why the prophets of Israel so violently attacked those they called false prophets, the ones who spoke smooth things, who prophesied illusions, who said, "Peace, peace!" when there was no peace at all (Jer. 23:9–40; Isa. 30:8–14). Prophets could normally be expected to speak words that challenged the operations and structures of the society. The prophets more often than not threatened a faithless people rather than praising a faithful one. The prophets pointed out the limits and weaknesses of the society, for that was their special function. Kings and princes always wished to control these voices of God, bending their will to the plans of the leaders. But the independent voice had to be maintained.

Of course, prophets of doom also could be perverse, could threaten harm from God and withdraw the threat for a price (note Amaziah's words to Amos in Amos 7:12–13). There were then no guarantees that a social critic was motivated only by commitment to the truth and to justice. All such words have to be weighed. But it is a sign of a healthy society when the voices of criticism and protest can be heard plainly and are not suppressed, and the health of the religious community can be gauged the same way.

It is possible to take heart about the situation today for this very reason. Never has there been more attention given to public wrongdoing. The crimes of those in high places are often identified and then shouted from the rooftops. Even though the result of such public hue and cry against evil is a loss of confidence in public officials and institutions, it is a tribute to the society's health that such misdeeds are as widely heralded as they are. Persons will bear false witness against the neighbor. Today, when they are found out, a host of neighbors hears of it almost immediately. It may be true that the public news media gives too much attention to such acts of misconduct and not enough to the signs of moral health and a morally sensitive society. But even so, the spotlight on human misdeeds can well reduce the misdeeds.

The same can be said about the widespread recognition that truth-telling often does more harm than good. We know much more clearly today that the motivation for speaking the truth can sometimes be malice, envy, spite, or hatred of the neighbor. But the commandment stands: false testimony before the community gravely damages the community. Indeed, the damage can prove fatal.

THE TENTH COMMANDMENT: NO LUSTING
AFTER THE LIFE OR GOODS OF OTHERS
"THOU SHALT NOT COVET THE
HOUSEHOLD OF THY NEIGHBOR"

In the tenth commandment the emphasis falls not first of all upon the deed done but upon the disposition of the self in the direction of the deed. The Hebrew word *ḥamad* means more than an attitude of desiring something and more than the powerful emotion of longing for something. It often has the meaning "to take steps to secure" something. See Prov. 1:22, where scoffers are asked how long they will continue to delight (Hebrew, *ḥameḏū*) in their scoffing, and Exod. 34:24, where we have God's promise that he will cast out the nations before Israel, enlarge her borders, and arrange matters so that no one shall desire (*ḥamad*) her land. The second passage apparently means that no one will be able to fulfill the desire for Israel's inheritance in the Promised Land, not that no one will ever desire to take possession of it.

It would be wrong, however, as we have noted earlier, to give to this verb a meaning that excludes the act of desiring, coveting, or lusting after. Some of the occurrences of the verb make a clear distinction between desiring something and the act of taking possession of it. One of the clearest instances is Josh. 7:20. There, Achan is finally led to confess his sin, giving glory to God as he tells the truth of his misdeed at Jericho. He says that when he saw certain rich objects among the spoils from Jericho he desired (*ḥamad*) them and took them and buried them under the floor of his tent. The desiring and the deed are closely related in Israelite thought, but they are not identical and not necessarily simultaneous acts.

It is often pointed out that in Deut. 5:21 (numbered 5:18 in some manuscripts) the word that follows the first verb, *ḥamad,* is the verb *'awah,* which unmistakably means to desire, to long for, to lust after. This verb does not exclude the making of plans to realize the desire, but neither does it require such activity. Thus we have additional support for the meaning of the verb with which this term, *'awah,* appears in parallelism in Deut. 5:21. *Ḥamad,* in short, can mean "desire," "covet," "lust after," and it does not always represent both the desire for something and the making of plans or taking of steps to secure the desired object.

Is there reason to suppose that a law dealing with the attitudes or the emotions, rather than the actual deeds, should be a too subtle or too refined religious notion for ancient Israel? One might grant that by the time of the Deuteronomist (seventh century B.C.) such a notion would be expected—after the work of Israel's great prophets and many of her great poets. But would early Israel have had a commandment against coveting? Some say no. The point is not that there was no concern for emotions or with the background of human action in early Israel, but rather that such a concern would normally not be regulated in Israelite law.

That is important. Israel was concerned with the deed rather than with the thought. So it was throughout Israelite history up to New Testament times. Public righteousness was a matter of actual faithfulness to God's Torah in word and in deed. The internal state of affairs of the individual would show itself in action, however, and was therefore of great importance for moral activity and for the shaping of the community's ethical norms and the attitude of community members to these norms. In such matters as love of the neighbor or hatred of the enemy the community of Israel recognized that the issue would be settled on the basis of actions that demonstrated love or hatred.

Even so, love was commanded for the neighbor (Lev. 19:18) and even for the stranger who dwelt within Israel (Lev. 19:34). To command love of God (Deut. 6:4) and of fellow human beings is to demand a kind of relationship and a quality of relationship between individuals and between groups that involves a "legislation" of one's feelings and thoughts and attitudes, although the test of the faithfulness to the command is given in discernible deeds displaying the thought or feeling or attitude.

In ancient Egypt there was a similar concern for the inner

qualities of human action and motivation, already in texts from the middle and late kingdoms (twentieth to mid-eighteenth centuries, and mid-sixteenth to twelfth centuries B.C.).[5] The tenth commandment's concern for lusting after the life and goods of others is thus not without precedent. Especially in the moral guidance of those being taught their duties in the society and at the court, such prohibitions as we have in the last five of the Ten Commandments often occupied a prominent place.

But just what did the tenth commandment wish to rule out? And how does this prohibition relate to the others, in particular the eighth and ninth commandments? It is probable that the focus of attention from early times was holding Israel firmly committed to Yahweh the God of the covenant. To live with no representations of the deity in plastic form was to live quite differently from most of Israel's neighbors. To observe every seventh day as a day of no work at all, simply stopping what one did normally, was not easily understood by the neighboring peoples; nor was it simple for Israel to do. We suspect that these two prohibitions in particular helped to produce in Israel a very common envy of those who *could* have plastic images of the deity and who *could* avoid the commitment to Sabbath observance. In this way the community was already being prepared to covet the *ways* of the neighboring peoples. A desire to be like the peoples of the surrounding cultures was an understandable temptation. It would be surprising if a desire to be like the other peoples should not have had an effect upon Israelite law.

It seems highly likely that this desire, this hankering after the ways of others, helped to lead the composer of the Decalogue to give attention to other forms of sick and dangerous desires. The hunger after a different kind of life would carry one over into the lust for the life of one's neighbors and for the neighbor's goods. Thus the prohibition may be a part of the Decalogue's purposed holding of the community and its individual members to the central place occupied by Israel in the world.

The detailed prohibitions, however, concentrate upon any unjustified interference in the life of the neighbor. No Israelite was to be caught up in lust for the goods of the neighbor—for his wife, for his animals, for anything at all that belonged to the neighbor. In the old curse ritual of Deuteronomy 27, the concern was with deeds done in secret, but here we are dealing with desires or attitudes that cannot initially be determined by anyone other than the desirer, the coveter. But the prohibition does not have the force of the curse; the curse was felt, by many at least, to work itself out automatically in the life of those who violated it. With regard to the Decalogue, the test of faithfulness to the commandment has to be worked out. As is the case throughout, the prohibitions of the Decalogue require the full panoply of Israelite legal tradition and administration, as well as the bodies of law produced over the centuries, for the actual administration of justice.

We still have to ask whether this commandment is not strikingly different from all the rest. In my judgment, it is not. The prohibition against coveting the life or goods of others is close to the prohibition against worship of any god other than Yahweh. The first commandment requires that no other divine being or principle count for anything in the life of the Israelite. Those who have associated themselves with the God of the covenant, with the God who brought Israel out of Egypt, are now bound to this God in interior ways. They give the allegiance of the heart to Yahweh and let no other divine or demonic realities in all the earth exercise any rival authority over them. They not only do not worship such other divine beings at the cult centers, but they give no credence to these powers, no place to such powers in their thinking or feeling.

Similarly, the Israelite is here and now required to keep himself from the power of lust for the neighbor's wife or possessions. Not only is he not to take the neighbor's wife as his own— which would be a violation of the seventh commandment—but he is also prohibited from lusting for the wife of the neighbor. It certainly does not rule out the appreciation of the beauty or other qualities of the wives of one's neighbors, nor is it a prohibition of the desire to have goods like those of a neighbor. The desire is thought of as beyond what is normal, a coveting of the other's goods that goes well beyond the desire to have one's own life enhanced by the possession of additional goods.

The emphasis falls upon coveting, however, not upon the person who owns the goods. The coveting of goods in the community that are set apart to Yahweh, for example, or that belong to the king and thus also to Yahweh, would be equally an act of coveting. Sick, perverse longings for the goods of others here fall under judgment. For that reason we need to be careful today to make it clear that when new or emerging nations, for example, long for the goods and qualities of life enjoyed by the more wealthy people of earth they are not necessarily violating the commandment not to covet. If the hunger for a life like that believed to exist in, say, the United States or Canada or West Germany should overwhelm and threaten to destroy a person from an African or Latin American land, then the commandment not to covet would come into play. But it would be entirely erroneous for the prohibition to be *used* by those who *have* an abundance of the goods of the earth to ward off the legitimate desires of the poor for a fairer share of those goods.

In fact, the commandment has been used in this way in times past. The use of other commandments or teachings that play down the significance of human life on this earth or the proper enjoyment of the goods of earthly life, when used by the "haves" to keep the "have-nots" contented with their lot is equally mistaken. Indeed, turning one's back on the materiality of contemporary life may be a misreading of this commandment, even when it is not at all intended to keep the less-well-provided parts of the earth in their place. This is one point at which biblical religion seems able to correct and put into sound perspectives certain other religious traditions (Buddhism, for example).[6]

Important as it is for contemporary men and women to find ways to overcome the surfeit of goods, of material possessions, in order to find what is of real value in life, it is also important that we not lose sight of the values of developed societies. Especially important are the developments in health, nutrition, and agriculture and the technological advances that ease the expenditure of physical labor. While we see clearly the new dangers and temptations that attend such "progress," we cannot reverse the movements in technological development without almost superhuman efforts. And we cannot insist that those persons who have not known the ennui of a life surfeited by goods and too much of food, drink, and other stimulations simply take our word for its shabbiness and worthlessness. Others might enhance the good and diminish the evil of these developments.

Does this commandment, then, have great import for our common life today? With all the dangers noted, is it not better to let the commandment remain in oblivion? I believe not. It is all too evident that human beings are bent upon envy, covetousness, and an unwholesome desire to take up the goods of life that surround them, whether such goods will be good for them or not. Ours is an age in which the appetite for more and more seems almost impossible to assuage. We find it increasingly difficult to maintain any sense of balance regarding our use of food; gadgets for home, office, or auto; clothing; entertainments done in our behalf as we look on; or recreational goods and equipment. Sometimes there is hardly time for envy or covetousness to operate consciously, since every desire seems to be met. Before the lust can do its destruction, the thing lusted after is ours.

Yet we know how virtually beyond being assuaged is the appetite for gadgets, food, pleasure, and luxuries. Indeed, it is the job of thousands upon thousands of our fellow citizens to see to it that the hunger for goods and yet more goods should never falter or dim. The very economic health of the world seems to depend upon ever-enlarging markets for goods that will be replaced by newly developed ones, on consumption that knows no bounds. Some persons therefore find it pernicious to talk about this tenth commandment in relation to the social and economic developments of a world community today.

I believe that the prohibition of destructive and overweening desires for the life and goods of others is entirely salutary today. Indeed, I think it necessary to distinguish unnatural and perverse desire for others' lives and goods from a deep hunger for a life that is wholesome, full, and good. Many of us really do not know what we want from the goods of life that are potentially available to us. In order to learn or relearn how to enjoy any of the goods of the earth it is necessary to sift our wants, to test them, to see which are born of envy or covetousness and which represent desires for which we are ready to labor and to make sacrifices, seeing the benefits to us and our families and friends.

When it is imperative for us as a human community to cut down on the waste of energy and other goods, when health itself demands a reform of eating habits, when labor is often felt to be without meaning, then the addressing of this commandment could have the widest-ranging consequences of any commandment. It may offer impetus to a sifting of desires to see which desires are in fact wholesome, which cannot possibly be realized without injustice or unfairness to others, and what in general would be a life lived this side of covetousness. Would it not be a glorious thing if we could test our appetites and desires to see which of them represent a hungering after more than we need or can use? We may thereby find that the most pervasive aspect of sin in our lives is the sin of overwhelming desire for more—not in relation to what other named individuals or groups have, but quite simply more. Where can there be any better check on adultery, stealing, bearing false witness, neglect of aged parents, neglect of Sabbath rest, misuse of God's power-filled name, idolatry, or the worship of false powers in the world? Were we able to help one another to temper and place in perspective our lust for . . . everything . . . we might begin to fall into step behind the God of the covenant.

PART THREE

THE TEN COMMANDMENTS
IN CHRISTIAN
PERSPECTIVE

CHAPTER 7

The Ten Commandments
and the
New Testament

JESUS AND THE TEN COMMANDMENTS

We do not intend to sketch the history of the Decalogue in later Israelite religious life, in the Jewish communities of postexilic times, or in early Christianity. Our concern is rather for the place of the Decalogue, and of such absolute demands from God as the Decalogue represents, in earliest Christianity. The part title indicates this limited focus, although we well understand how difficult it may be today to determine Jesus' view of the authority and place of the Ten Commandments in the life of those who were most closely associated with him.

It will be necessary, however, to give some picture of the developments in Israel prior to Jesus' time. Textually, the most striking developments are two: (1) the additions to the commandments and the subtractions from their original form that we can see in the versions of the Decalogue in Exodus and in Deuteronomy; and (2) the existence of these two versions. We have commented briefly on these two points earlier. Let us add only that both the additions and the subtractions are very much in the spirit of the Deuteronomic tradition of the eighth and seventh centuries, that tradition of Levitical witness to Israelite faith which flourished in many towns and villages in Israel, was given to practical teaching of Torah, and was heavily indebted to the great prophets of Israel'for its understandings. Indeed, we can say that the Deuteronomic and Deuteronomistic traditions decisively influenced Israelite law, and the Decalogue as well.[1]

It is my contention that the Decalogue was the first part of the old covenant law that was to some considerable extent loosed from the cult and from Israelite worship to become an "independent entity," as Martin Noth called it.[2] But I contend, against Noth's central thesis in this regard, that such a development was a part of the very intention of early Israelite thought regarding the Decalogue, and with respect to Torah as such; it was not, as Noth maintained, a regrettable development that followed upon the destruction of the city of Jerusalem in 587 B.C.

This intention was obscured and compromised by later developments of law in the two kingdoms and was clarified by the Deuteronomic Levites and by the final Deuteronomistic historian or historians. Noth claimed that when the law was loosed from its moorings in a vital stream of cultic activity, after Jerusalem fell in 587 B.C., the way was prepared for law to become an independent entity, destined to develop into a sterile system of commands and prohibitions of the sort against which Jesus protested. Torah became law with all the negative associations of that term that developed in Christianity and that the apostle Paul attacked so vehemently.

The law of Israel did suffer in the course of historical developments. An unwholesome legalism is one of the constant religious temptations and dangers, especially acute in a "religion of the book," where the requirements can be set down precisely. But the Ten Commandments are a force *against* such legalism, not in support of it. Indeed, the existence of law in the sense of absolute prohibitions that cannot be broken is the precondition for freedom and for joy and responsible life in a community of free persons (see Chapter 8).

The prophets knew this very well. Their catalogs of the violations of covenant occasionally singled out several of the Ten Commandments, and in other instances the prologue was probably quoted as a reminder of the contents of the Decalogue as a whole. Other catalogs of crimes or of exemplary acts of faithfulness to Yahweh developed by analogy with the list of ten very distinctive ones, those taught to children at an early age and remembered by reference to the ten fingers.

In Deuteronomy, however, a very special context is created for the continuing observance of the Decalogue, a context and an ideological interpretation of it that make the Decalogue, and faithfulness to it, a touchstone for membership in the community of Israel. This context appears in the narrative material that precedes and follows the Deuteronomic legal collection as such. Of special importance are chaps. 4, 29, and 30. Chapter 4 in particular offers the remarkable view that God gave the commandments orally to Moses, from the midst of the fire on Mount Horeb. The flaming fire assured that there was no form of God there visible or even present. God gave the Decalogue in words only, through a voice only, and once Moses had received that oral law, which was the ten words themselves, he had only to put it on the two tablets of stone. The recording on stone, and the later writing of the commandments on leather or papyrus or potsherds, would be allowed, but such written forms of the Decalogue were derivative. The Decalogue was understood, by this rather late (late seventh or early sixth century B.C.) tradition or individual, to be essentially vocal, spoken, deriving from God's own voice from the flaming fire of the mountain of revelation.

Such a tradition was certainly intended to underscore several important points. First, the Ten Commandments were to be committed to memory by every Israelite and kept alive in the heart. We do not know when such a tradition and practice might first have developed or how long or in what ways it was passed on from one generation to the next. But it certainly seems to be presupposed by this passage in Deuteronomy 4. Second, this basic summation of Torah was capable of being kept. That fundamental view of the Deuteronomistic writer needs underscoring. The commands were not an impossible ideal, designed only to be approximated and used as a norm to show us how far short we fall of the ideal. These Deuteronomistic traditions at least insist that the Decalogue is not only such an ideal but an ideal capable of being incorporated into life.

Third, the commands themselves were not to be understood or employed in such a way as to violate the commands them-

selves, especially the first three. God alone was God—not Torah.
God would brook no rivals, not even Torah. And treating Torah
as other than the voice from the fire, requiring fidelity to Him
whose voice spoke the Torah, would not be allowed, on penalty
of death. Also, the words of Torah could not be used to do damage or violence to others in God's name. Israel did not control
these words, and she does not now control them. Freely God
spoke from the flames; Moses could only hear and heed, and
then record the "ten words."

Fourth, these words were continually alive, were near, were
vital links between the God of the covenant and his people.
They were not far off, not a part of a tradition grown cold. They
were words still having within and around them the heat of
God's breath. These are words that sink deeply into the heart of
the people and of each of its members, as close to the inner self
of every Israelite as anything can possibly be. *God* is thereby
known to be present within the interior self, known as the Lord,
and known in the way Jeremiah prophesied would one day occur
(Jer. 31:31–34).

Fifth, these words mark the paths that lead, respectively, to
death and to life. They clearly lay out the way of death, the way
on which all who do what is here prohibited are embarked. This
way of death, however, is not marked by immediacy, and the
death does not follow by virtue of the doing of the misdeed,
automatically, as once the curse brought its threatened judgment
to pass. And neither is this path one that Israel's judges and
elders first point out; the Lord first pointed it out through the
voice speaking these very words from the fire.

Such words also point out the path that means life, good,
blessing. Israel is in the situation of choice always, not only on
particular occasions but every day of her life. She is to choose
life, for that is the only choice that is meaningful, desirable, ra-
tional (Deut. 30:11–20). The voice from the flame pointed out
the way that leads surely to death, in God's own way and time,
and the converse of that way is the way to life and blessing.
Israel has one choice: to choose life. The other possibility is not
excluded, but it is an utterly self-defeating option, the clear sign

that the one who spoke from the flames of the fire of revelation atop the mountain has not yet found a way to accomplish his purpose for those to whom he spoke. He warns of exile and sends it if he must, but he will not forever be put in the position of judge. He will one day circumcise the heart, will turn the judgment away from a repentant people, will have finally a people who love him with all their heart. But the people will have to call to mind these words from the fire. They will have to return to the Lord and obey his voice. This oral law, this living voice of God, can be resisted, but it is madness to do so. Only death can follow, and God wills the gifts of life and blessing and health for his people, and not their opposite.

From this quick survey of the rich outlook of our Deuteronomistic historian we get a marvelous picture of what Torah was best seen to mean in the Jewish community of Jesus' day.[3] Jesus must have been steeped in the Deuteronomic tradition. In the Gospels in their present form, there are seventy-seven quotations from the Book of Deuteronomy alone. Jesus' quotation from the Deuteronomic Shema gives immense prominence to this tradition of Israel (Matt. 22:34–40; Mark 12:28–34; Luke 10:25–28). And the Sermon on the Mount is best understood formally as a recapitulation of the words of God from the flame, just such a recapitulation as we have in Deuteronomy from the mountains of Moab. It is Deuteronomy and not Exodus that is the best counterpart and foil for the Sermon on the Mount. Indeed, the beginning of the Sermon with blessings rather than the ending of the laws with curses and blessings is probably a deliberate reversal of the layout of the Book of Deuteronomy, carried through by the writer-editor of the Gospel of Matthew.

The analogy with Moses and with Deuteronomy is close indeed and could be extended: beginning of the recapitulation in the wilderness; address to the people from the mountainside; recognition of the decisive break that lies just ahead—the time of consummation; selection of those to carry on the work; warnings of the consequences of apostasy or faintheartedness; and of course the coming death of the giver of the words. But the most striking point has to do with Jesus' understanding of the Torah,

the Decalogue, and all that issues from it. It is the living word
of the Gospel, the very truth of God. It means life and health
for all; it is inexhaustible in its richness, but plain for all to
understand; it can be kept; and it sets forth the two ways unmistakably. We can immediately see that it would be a travesty
of interpretation to make Jesus the enemy of Torah in the sense
of the Decalogue and its fundamental requirements. The positive form of the Decalogue is the Shema and the neighbor-law of
Lev. 19:18. But the Decalogue itself gives us a summary of what
Israel and humankind dare not fail to observe, even though they
have the freedom to do so.

Jesus quotes from the Ten Commandments on only one stated
occasion, according to the Gospels (Matt. 19:16–22; Mark 10:
17–22; Luke 18:18–30). Each of the three listings differs from
the other two, and neither of the listings includes all ten of the
commandments. Jesus apparently selected just those that were
most weighty for rich persons to bear in mind: killing, adultery,
stealing, false witness, honoring of parents. The differences in
the order of the commandments may suggest that the identification of one finger of the hand with one of the ten commandments was no longer common, if it had ever been. But such a
view is not necessarily supported by the variations in the order.
It could well be that Jesus' response, while not casual, is intended to mention several but not all of the commandments as
instances of what he meant by "Keep the commandments!"

There is, however, another element in this story from the
Gospels that is particularly striking. According to two of the
accounts, Jesus rejected the epithet "good" in the designation
"good teacher," saying that God alone is to be called good.
Keeping of the commandments does not make one deserving of
the epithet "good," and that means that the keeping of the
commandments is recognized by Jesus to be more than a matter
of morality, more than conformity to ethical norms. To keep
the commandments is to live as a child of the Kingdom, to be a
committed member of the people of the covenant. Or, in the
words of·Deuteronomy, one must hear and heed the voice of
God from the flames, a voice announcing the new day that is

now dawning, the new and open possibilities of life that burst forth from this day of fulfillment and consummation. It is to decide here and now for the new Torah.

The special teaching of Jesus, according to Matthew's account of the Sermon on the Mount (Matthew 5-7), contains several connections with the Decalogue and involves what at first appears to be a sharp contrast to it. But closer examination of these stated qualities of life in the Kingdom show that both in the Decalogue and here there are more similarities than differences. Jesus portrays a set of activities and actions to be avoided that intensify the rigorous demands placed upon the citizen of God's kingdom. And much greater place is given the situation of those who are victimized by the strong and powerful and who hold fast to their commitment to God and to fellow human beings in the face of such distress. More emphasis may fall upon the inner qualities that express themselves in the deed than upon the deed alone. Even so, the special teaching of Jesus is consistent with the prohibitions of the Decalogue, carrying forward their contents.

Note the following examples: Not only is one not to kill (the sixth commandment), but one is not to be torn apart with anger, not to curse the brother or the sister, not to use contemptuous language to or about anyone (Matt. 5:21-22). Not only is one not to commit adultery (the seventh commandment), but one is to avoid lustful looks, for such lusting in advance of the act of adultery is adultery in the heart (Matt. 5:27-30). Not only is one not to bear false witness against the neighbor (the ninth commandment), but one is not to use oaths at all and instead quite simply state the facts of the case truthfully and with economy of speech (Matt. 5:33-37).

In Luke's account of the Sermon on the Mount (Luke 6:17-49) none of these direct references to the Decalogue appears. Instead, the inner qualities of life in the Kingdom are found without the contrasts stated in Matthew's Gospel. But in Matthew, too, we cannot fail to recognize that Jesus builds upon the Decalogue and indeed presupposes the truth and continuing validity of it. When he speaks about what one has heard from the sages of ancient time, the evangelist Matthew has in view not the Torah in the narrow sense but certain interpretations of Torah that Jesus (like several of his predecessors and contemporaries and successors among the sages of Israel) finds not sufficiently rigorous.

LAW AND GOSPEL

The relation of Jesus, Paul, and early Christianity to the Decalogue that is most important for our purposes appears in another connection. It is not the matter of God's basic requirements of life in the Kingdom that is the fundamental difference between Judaism and Christianity in the first Christian century. Nor is it the issue of whether the Decalogue is a good summary of such requirements. The great difference lies at two points that will be of immense importance in the later history of the relations between Judaism and Christianity. They are (1) the question of how Gospel and Law are related to one another within Christianity and (2) how this relationship affects the relation between Judaism and Christianity.[4] We will not be able to say much of contemporary value about the Decalogue in the Christian community if we do not shed some light on and deal directly with these two issues.

The two matters are enormously complex and difficult to understand. They touch upon the essential mystery of Christian faith, focusing in a striking way upon the presence and the work of God in Jesus Christ. It is not difficult to sum up the traditional answer to these issues. It would run somewhat like this:

In the time of Jesus, it is said, Judaism had become more and more a religion marked by punctilious observance of a Torah that, especially in the interpretation of the Pharisees and their associates the scribes, sought to regulate and control the whole of Israel's life. To their credit, the Pharisees were bent upon *interpreting* Torah's requirements for all of practical life, for Torah was not merely to be given lip service, it was to be *obeyed*. But, it is claimed, Torah had become a weighty and oppressive burden for the people, a religion of detailed commands and prohibitions covering every conceivable aspect of the common life, requiring joyless and lifeless conformity with un-challengeable norms laid down and interpreted by the experts in Torah.

Jesus broke all that, as John the Baptist before him had begun to do. Jesus saw a time of fulfillment of the hopes and longings of humankind that had now come to pass: the signs of fulfillment and newness of life in the Kingdom were there for those with eyes of faith to see. The central message of God for this day of consummation is love, new life in association with God, a fresh joy and peace and blessedness in the Kingdom which is being consummated within Israel here on earth. No longer need God's people be burdened by anxiety over whether they might have violated the requirements of Torah; let them repent of their misdeeds and failings and joyously turn to God. Life in the Kingdom begins here and now. It requires a break with the old life and its ways, a renunciation of mere observances of Torah, mere lip service to the Kingdom's demands, mere fol-lowing along in the way the tradition has pointed out. Although the demands are strenuous ("You shall be perfect!"), the yoke of the Kingdom can be borne lightly by those who, casting off the burden of conventional observances, follow Jesus into the new life and fellowship of the Kingdom.

Many Jews heard and heeded this message, among them a high percentage of the poor and the oppressed of Galilee and Judaea, along with several influential Jewish leaders. But for the majority there was no acceptance of the message of Jesus. Rather, the community of Israel saw in Jesus' message a prema-ture or unjustified claim concerning the Kingdom. Jesus claimed that fulfillment of life in the coming Kingdom was already at hand, already freeing people for life in the new age and freeing them from their bondage to the Torah's formal requirements, cere-monies, usages. The claim was not supported by the facts. Those who associated themselves with Jesus might well *believe* that in the inner life which they shared with him and with one another such a new joy in God was at hand, a new freedom from Torah, and a new delight in the knowledge of God's love and acceptance. But it was an inward kind of thing, not really comparable with what Jewish thinkers had promised as characteristic of this expected Day of Consummation.

Judaism, then, in its main branches rejected Christianity as another sectarian movement without fundamental truth to it, just as it rejected various apocalyptic movements, Essene sectarian withdrawal from life, and the most violent and excessive forms of political messianism. Jewish interpreters have often been willing to affirm the power of Jesus' interpretations of Torah, the freshness and vigor of his approach to life, the remarkable qualities that made him one of the greatest of the founders of religion known to the world. But they have had to reject Christianity because, especially as a result of the work of Paul the theologian, Christianity became a religion of redemption *from* the world, an otherworldly religion, rather than a consummation of the promise of God to his people Israel.[5]

And Christian interpreters often have gone on to see in the developments of Christianity after the death of Jesus an inevitable break with Judaism. Now, in the face of the resurrection of Jesus from death, God has said "No!" not only to the power of death to claim all life and its values but also to the Jewish community that did not accept Jesus, indeed put him to death, or collaborated in that death. This picture is then often extended to show that the commitment to Torah by Jews who rejected Jesus was a commitment to a religion in which obedience, law, judgment, and stern righteous demand were at the heart and center.[6] Small wonder that God chose the Christian community as the "New Israel" (an expression not found in the New Testament!) and rejected his faithless and unbelieving "Old Israel."

This outlook went so far, for example in the case of Marcion, as to call for a rejection of the "Old" Testament with its oppressive God and the acceptance as Scripture of a refined and purified "New" Testament. And even when Marcion lost out and the entire Bible of contemporary Christianity was retained, the outlook of Marcion often prevailed. It was of course the case that Jews in early times persecuted the new movement and sought to eradicate it, just as, later on, Christianity retaliated by attempting to eradicate Judaism.

We can understand the extreme difficulty of an interpreter of Christian faith such as the apostle Paul when we see how the question of the consummation of God's work in Jesus—the Christ whom God raised from death and established as Lord— had to be interpreted in connection with the broad outlines of Jewish history and thought. It was a staggeringly difficult task for one who held firmly to his Jewish existence and at the same time could not deny that he had undergone a new birth into Christ Jesus and was now a new creation. Among the many ramifications of his discussions and polemics with fellow Jews and with Gentiles, the question of Torah loomed large indeed. For Paul, the Torah was good and wholesome and intended to be life-giving and life-supporting. But sin entered the world— with the first human pair, before Torah had been given—and with sin came death, death to the life in communion with God that God purposed all along. After sin had appeared, Paul came to see, Torah as the good gift of a good and gracious God, which always remained just such a good gift of God's grace, would inevitably fall upon human beings not only as grace but also as a demand that sinful humankind could not fully or adequately maintain. Therefore a Torah that was *not* sin became, in its effectual out-workings, the instrument through which I came to recognize sin as sin. Without Torah there would be no sin; there would be only moral wrongdoing, not sin against God's holiness and justice and love.[7]

But such a meaning for Torah is by no means negative. Sin is the negative reality, the destructive force, the act of turning from God and damaging or breaking the relation between Lord and creature. Sin enters the picture to demonstrate that God will not have his people fall into danger, destructiveness, and death. He will have them live. Torah points the way, gives guidance, shows to others also the way when the faithful in their midst follow Torah.

When Torah is flouted it is no longer a matter of failings or moral turpitude, of death that comes fatefully; it is a matter of action by God's people against God. It is sin against God, and that prompts action by God, not merely the emergence of certain inevitable consequences that lie in the chain of cause and effect. Paul recognized this critical function of sin and saw its pedagogic value—it led one to Christ.[8] For Jews not drawn to accept this view, however, Torah still has this drawing power. It enables one to know who one is, what God will have in the world, where lies the course of life that leads to joy and peace and blessedness.

There is a negative side to revelation, of course. Paul also knew that until the Torah came there was not the same seriousness about the state of the world, life, or purpose in life. It was possible for human beings apart from the gift of Torah knowingly to fail in their responsibilities to God, for by virtue of their very creation God planted in them a minimal consciousness of the way in which their lives were to go (Rom. 1:18–23). But far more serious was the lot of those who belonged, or came by divine grace and their own decision to belong, to the people of God, knowing the demands of Torah, knowing sin for what it was and knowing Christ's gracious act for our redemption, God's action through Christ for our redemption, and the new life. For those touched by grace and drawn into the ambit of Christ's love in this distinctive way, the situation of the Torah, when rejected, is all the more grave. Now a knowing death comes; now there is a wretchedness about life and oneself never known before; now life becomes truly unbearable, a misery so deep that it is death in the midst of life. That is to say, Torah works to open before our eyes the jaws of death and hell, to show us the impossibility of continuing on the course of faithlessness to Torah. This is the misery of one touched by grace who then sees how his or her actions in the kingdom of grace seem a travesty of those intended; seeing the good, we do not do it; seeing evil and knowing its deathly poison, we still are drawn to take that poison. Wretched ones that we are, who can deliver us from this body of death (Rom. 7:24)?

The Christian knows who. There is no longer the final, irretrievable condemnation that follows from such a reaction to God's gift of Torah and to the attendant demands of Torah. There is now the deepened awareness of the yawning chasm opening beneath the feet of the one who spurns Torah. But God's grasp upon the knowing sinner, or the one tempted to sin, is firm and entirely reliable. Now we are freed from the anxious striving to keep Torah at all costs lest we perish. But the incentive to keep Torah is deeper than ever before, deeper than any promptings of dread or fear or gnawing anxiety. The Torah is kept because God summons us to do so, and we want to do what God wants us to do because we want to sustain the relation of love, the quality of joy and blessedness in being, that faithfulness to Torah entails and produces.

In some such way we have to see the relation of Jesus to the Ten Commandments. He is utterly faithful to Torah, indeed without sin, according to Christian tradition. Yet he lives a full life in this world of corruption, sin, anxiety, and wretchedness. The New Testament offers many images and statements to express this identification of Jesus with sinful humankind and with the world under sin's power, an identification that is at once complete and yet not productive of sin. However such a paradox is to be dealt with, the New Testament shows a Jesus who is both under the Torah and free in relation to it. He fulfills its requirements and helps persons the better to see just what those requirements entail. Yet he is never overwhelmed by the requirements, never driven to anxiety by them, lest he somehow fail God, and never ready to let merely formal adherence to the demands of Torah get in the way of the fulfillment of the deeper purposes and intentions of God through the Torah.

Jesus thus becomes an example par excellence for the observance of Torah's prohibitions and of the kind and quality of life implicit in those prohibitions. If we look back at the Old Testament literature, however, we see many other such examples. The prophets attacked Israel for the worship of other gods, for idolatry, for misuse of God's name, for neglect of the responsibility for true and authentic worship and for authentic and faithful life in community. But they also attacked the people for merely formal Sabbath observance that was not a part of true commitment to God and to fellow Israelites—just as sharply as Jesus did (see, e.g., Amos 8:5; Isa. 1:13).

Christian faith, then, depends as much upon the recognition of the true place of Torah as it does upon the recognition of the true place of God's gracious coming to us in love. When we now look back at the two matters we set out to illuminate in this section, both seem to be somewhat clarified. The relation between Law and Grace is one in which we do not dare play one off against the other. And the relation between Christianity and Judaism is seen as one in which both depend upon both Torah and divine grace. Law *is* seen in Christianity to be *both* the undoing of the person being claimed by grace *and* the depth-dimension of the life in grace. And in Christianity there is an insistence that the transforming day of grace has come so near, has taken such a firm hold upon the world and its peoples through God's actions in Jesus Christ, that observance of Torah is now transposed into a new key. The struggle between Judaism and Christianity, both intellectually and spiritually, continues on just this central issue of Torah—its meaning, its relation to God's love, its relation to the destiny of Israel and to the vocation of Israel in the world.

Let us not, however, fail to recognize that the message of the Christian gospel is a message of liberation and glory in the world that is not exhausted by an identification of how Torah, or the Decalogue, appears within it. The sense of joy and excitement that permeates the New Testament literature arises from a disclosure concerning the very meaning and possibility of life in the world as such. It has to do with a relationship that is recognized as centering in God's raising Jesus from death, a relationship that transfigures every aspect of human life, all dimensions of sin and suffering, all elements of personal and social existence in the political structures. Human beings touched by the mystery of God's love in Jesus Christ do indeed live by Torah as God's gift, but they do so with a confidence in life, a joy in relation to God's good and transformed earth, and a hope for the resolution of all the tragic dimensions of life that seem to go beyond even the eschatological anticipations of Israel's prophets. Life is now life in the Spirit, where the Jesus who died and was raised by God is present to his community in the

Spirit. And with that presence, the whole Christian community receives all the gifts of God, including Torah, in association with the central Gift.[9]

There thus develops a greater emphasis on thanksgiving or, better, praise-giving as the central note in Christian prayer and worship. All that comes to the community comes in this context of praise-giving, or eucharist. Torah is the same gift of a gracious God that it was for ancient Israel and for the Jewish community of the first Christian century that did not accept Christ as the Savior. But faithfulness to Torah within the Christian community is marked by a fresh and awesome sense of the mystery of a love of God that would not withhold even the Son from a world groaning for redemption. Fidelity to the demand of God for the Christian community is marked by a deepened sense of the unfathomable depths of the love with which God loved the world that had spurned Torah.

The two communities, therefore, do have an equally high regard for God's Torah. Commandment looms large in both, and commandment is premised in both on the grace and love of the God who lays down commands. But the Jewish community that does not enter into the Christian community (and by far the largest percentage of the Jewish community does not do so) has one powerful witness to the Christian community then and through the subsequent centuries. It witnesses to the need to see more clearly and unmistakably, in the public world, the signs of the consummation of God's purposes for the world and humankind. Christianity, on its part, is required to witness to the Jewish community concerning a consummation that is real and discernible, even if not yet the publicly visible reality that God calls for. It is a matter of the *extent* to which Christianity can claim in truth that the consummation of God's love and grace, and the new demands that ensue, is anticipated in this present age. Or, put in terms applicable concretely to the Jewish community, it is a matter of the readiness of the Jewish community to recognize and acknowledge the extent to which the consummation is already present, before its full and final display. Judaism witnesses against a faithless Christianity or a triumphalist

Christianity that claims more than its actual life supports. And Christianity may be able, when faithful, to witness against a Judaism that should be able to discern the consummation that God indeed has brought near.

How different this way of relating Judaism and Christianity is from that of relating the two on the basis of a rigid distinction between Law and Gospel! There is Gospel in Judaism and there is Law in Christianity. There is also anticipation of the kingdom of God in both communities. The Christian community is bold enough to claim a kind and quality of life in the Kingdom that the Jewish community is not willing to claim. Therein is a major difference, one never to be overlooked. But a renewed effort on the part of the Christian community to appreciate and reclaim its heritage of Torah should greatly help to enable the two communities to focus their disagreements on the central realities that in fact do distinguish them from one another.

CHAPTER 8

The Ten Commandments
in Religious
Life Today

In this closing chapter we hope to bring together in a systematic way the findings of the study thus far. We hope also to indicate how these efforts to understand the Decalogue may point the way for a reassessment of the relations of Judaism and Christianity and the import of these two biblical religions for contemporary understanding: religious, humanistic, or atheistic. The chapter can only provide pointers, largely in the form of theses briefly elucidated. Readers will be able to see how the systematic study relates to the prior exegetical and historical work. Much work remains to be done on systematic biblical ethics. I hope that this set of studies will prove helpful as the concentration on ethics in Israelite and early Christian literature proceeds—a rather new development, which I welcome very much.[1]

Our thought is grouped under three headings: (1) bondage under God, (2) freedom under God, and (3) the Ten Commandments: charter of human freedom.

BONDAGE UNDER GOD

The Ten Commandments, and indeed the general religious outlook of the Jewish people, show us the need always to keep together freedom and bondage. I use the stronger term, "bondage," because such terms as "order" or "obligation" or "structure" are insufficient designators of the sense of sacral obligation to the God of Israel, a God known by name and known to have taken full possession of the slaves whom he had redeemed from

173

bondage in Egypt. And bondage also points to a master, which makes it a term more suitable than "necessity" or "providence" or other abstract designations.

We saw in the additions to Deuteronomy how the Ten Commandments were personalized, related to the living voice of God. Now we need to look at the prophetic sense of obligation to Yahweh that is one of the expressions of the Israelite recognition of bondage to God. Amos is particularly helpful with his picture of God's election of the people to service in and for the world of God's creation. After his catalog of the crimes of the nations of the Syrian-Palestine region (chaps. 1–2) he points to God's special tie to Israel: "You alone have I known from among all the families of earth; as a result, I visit upon you all your iniquities!" (Amos 3:2)

God's choice of his people Israel binds that people to God in a way that is at once a burden, a mystery, and a joy. The ancient generations of Israelites, and some among modern and contemporary Jewish communities, might make the mistake of concentrating upon the privilege involved in the election of Israel. Not so Amos or the other prophets. They know the joy of intimate association with One who holds life together, discloses its purposes, assures meaning and direction, acceptance and love. Small wonder that this intimate sense of God's love for his people, especially underscored in Hosea, Deuteronomy, and Jeremiah, should now and again have led to an overstatement of God's favor for this people, his determination in a time to come to avenge them by destroying their enemies or by causing the enemy peoples to lavish treasures upon God's favored ones. But such a development is under constant pressure of prophetic voices that speak differently.[2]

It is this difference that deserves the designation "bondage under God." Already the older narratives recognized the obligation that followed from God's election. We saw it in the prologue to the Decalogue (Exod. 20:2), and it is found in the narrative bridge of the Yahwistic tradition that connects the primeval history (Genesis 1–11) with the story of the patriarchs (Genesis 12–35), namely, in Gen. 12:1–3. The command to leave family and homeland for a new and unnamed land that Yahweh will point out to Abraham includes the expression "and *be* a blessing!" (12:2). The promise to Abram (as he is here called) is tied not only to the command to leave home and follow Yahweh but also to the command to be the blessing to others that he is promised he will be.[3]

Also, it is unmistakable that early narrative writers saw how absolutely indispensable to Israel's future was the continuing presence of the demanding God Yahweh, the one who wrought deliverance from Egyptian bondage and who jealously guarded the life of those delivered, protecting them from the dangers that threatened Israel's very life and also scrutinizing Israel's life to see how the people measured up. This last point is the one that produces the almost pathological sense of obligation to Yahweh that we find in the prophets. Israel is fated, or one might almost say doomed, to be held to account by Yahweh. Never in human history has such a development occurred before or again, so far as one can determine. This sense of a "metaphysical" obligation to Yahweh is apparently not prompted by gratitude for deliverance. More important is the sense of fear and dread that derives from the ancient, almost primeval, sense of Yahweh's holiness and jealous concern for his own people. Primitive religious understandings seem to have been transmuted into a sense of the moral obligation to hold fast to God's covenant. Fear is by no means absent, but fear of the consequences for oneself is certainly not the appropriate way to describe this sense of the awesome need to be faithful to Yahweh.

It seems probable that, especially from the time of Amos forward, the election of Israel is understood by some thinkers in Israel as an election to practice the kind of faithfulness to the moral will of God on which the very continued existence of the world and all human society depends. Just as in the more fertility-oriented aspects of ancient Near Eastern worship the very health of the world depends upon the renewal of life and fertility in and through the cult and those cultic acts that enable people to participate with God in such cosmic renewal, so now, in Israel's prophetic religion, the very continuation of life on earth depends upon fidelity to the will of God in social, economic, cultural, and cultic actions and relations. The cheating of persons in business, the befouling of family relations, the corruption of justice in the courts, acts of violence against the neighbor, contempt for God's gifts in general—these are, to Amos, signs that Yahweh is certain to bring an early end to Israel's life and, in all likelihood, to human life as such. Such a failure on Israel's part is the greater precisely because so much depends upon Israel's being a firm and clear model of public righteousness before the nations. What is going on in the capital towns of the surrounding peoples is bad indeed; it reveals a wanton disregard for life and a spread of violence that is terribly dangerous. God's fire will thus break out soon to sweep away such evil and cleanse the place where it was. But for *Israel* to be engaged in such crimes—that is for life itself to be threatened with extinction. If the very source of moral understanding for the world has been corrupted and polluted, how can there be any hope for an amendment of the ways of humankind in general? It is fairly clear that Amos sees the threat to Israel as much more serious for the world than the threat to other peoples. Were Israel to have to be destroyed, as seemed possible to him, another people would need to be called by God to fulfill the vocation of Israel in the world (Amos 9:7). It is probable, however, that Amos did not anticipate the utter destruction of God's people: fragments (perhaps Amos bitterly chose to point to virtually worthless fragments; Amos 3:12) might be left; "perhaps" God would be gracious to the remnant of Joseph (5:15). If vv. 9–10 of chap. 9 are from Amos, as I believe them to be, then Amos on one occasion at least spoke of a terrible shaking and sifting of Israel among the nations, a testing that *all* would have to undergo, after which God's people would have yet another opportunity to show their faithfulness to Yahweh and to fulfill their vocation on behalf of the nations.

It is the positive side of this bondage of Israel that helps to complete the picture. The prophets of Israel came to an understanding of historical process that was of immense value in keeping the sense of bondage to God and his demands from being or becoming abstract or enslaving. Not only did the prophets hold the people to account to keep the Torah, in the conviction that a failure of such obedience meant ruin for the world, but some of these prophets—notably Hosea, Isaiah, Micah, Jeremiah, Ezekiel and 2 Isaiah—came to the judgment that Israel would in fact not forever be able to thwart God's promised blessing for her and for the nations.[4] Although these prophets did not speak of this time of consummation, this fulfillment of God's purpose and promise, in identical terms or with equal frequency, all of them were convinced that God's people were being drawn forward to a day of the Lord that would be the fulfillment of God's plans. This time of consummation depended, in a sense, upon Israel's faithfulness to God; such faithfulness would usher in the day and was therefore felt and understood to be the only right and proper course of action by Israel—individual Israelites as well as the people as a whole. But the astonishing development was that these few prophets (and no doubt many, many others in ancient Israel) were drawn to believe that this time of consummation was near at hand and would surely come, almost in defiance of Israel's sin.

It appears that these prophets came to the view that Yahweh refused to tolerate the sin of his people to the extent that the world would forever remain in its misery. Yahweh would have his day of consummation, even if it required an almost feverish forgiveness of Ephraim's sin (Hos. 11:7–9), an act of tearing out a heart of stone and replacing it with a heart of flesh (Ezek. 36:26–27), the giving of a new covenant that meant the end of the need for Torah itself to be taught (Jer. 31:31–34). Whatever the condition of Zion today—harlot city, faithless and obdurate, supine before the foreign tyrant, in ruins and its temple smoking from the flames—Zion would inevitably be the center of the universe, the place where peace and tranquillity would finally be centered, both for Israel and for the foreign powers.[5] Again, it should be noted that these prophets *expected* their hearers to see the point of this sure determination of God to fulfill his promises to all the families of earth, including Israel; they wanted the hearers *immediately* to begin to live the faithful life appropriate to the day and the place of consummation. We may be sure that many did so, that many *were* drawn to be faithful to Torah and to Yahweh in new and fresh ways, in light of these glorious and often-repeated and celebrated promises. We may also be sure that the bondage to God was cemented by such visions of a certain time of consummation that God had appointed.

How did this prophetic eschatology bind the people to God—those people, that is, who took it seriously? It was the simple but profoundly supportive conviction that God would be true to his promise that tied the believing members of the community to God. Such a conviction seemed to call further into question and to condemn the kind of conduct or indeed the kind of attitude that was itself a denial that God's purposes would come to fulfillment. When people depended upon alliances with other world powers for their security they thereby denied that Yahweh had the course of human history under his sway. When they made Zion into a harlot city, again they denied that Zion was on the way to becoming the faithful city, the city on the hill to whom the nations were being drawn to learn God's Torah and commit themselves to the practices of peace.[6]

This conviction also gave confidence in the midst of trials and destruction and despair. No matter what might be the situation of God's people in the world at any given time, the faithful were able to say that God's justice and God's peace would not always be deferred or delayed. God was faithful to his promise, even though God's faithfulness was a conviction of faith, not a bland or self-evident teaching in the manner of portions of Israel's wisdom teaching. Such a conviction can indeed be bland or blind, and can encourage individuals or groups simply to wait quietly for God to intervene to save and restore one's fortunes. It can also easily fit in with a too ready acknowledgment of sin and a groveling before God in a humility that is degrading. Alternatively, it can be born of a too ready conviction that one's cause is right and certain to be supported by God, thus allowing neither for prophetic criticism nor for self-criticism.

But in relative freedom from such dangers a prophetic eschatology that affirms the near and sure triumph of God's purposes can be a powerful binding force, enabling persons and groups to know and to feel that their lives are sure and secure in God. God holds them, and nothing can break that hold.

Is this a real sense of being bound to God? Is it a form of human bondage? And if so, is it also a sense of bondage under Torah? Is it the kind of bondedness that we claim was felt to hold the people to the Decalogue and its summary requirements? I believe that the answer to these questions is affirmative. In ancient Israel there developed, in partial dependence upon Moses' own religious discoveries, a recognition of bondage to Yahweh deeper than any sense of being bound to the terms of the covenant, by analogy with ancient Near Eastern treaties. Such a recognition was also deeper than fear of attack by Yahweh who laid down arbitrary laws that one dare not challenge, and deeper than any sense of gratitude for favors bestowed.

It is a sense of kinship, of family ties, of life entwined with life, of a kind of destiny that awaits and is running its course toward a goal being realized. Moses is to say to the Pharaoh, "Israel is my first-born son . . . Let my son go that he may serve me" (Exod. 4:22–23). Israel is a son, but a son who serves God and is bound to God in service just as deeply as Israel once was bound to the Pharaoh. It is not merely the obligation that derives from gratitude for deliverance. It is not even right to say that it is obligation issuing from love—although that is profoundly the case as well. Something deeper lies here, something more mysterious, more a part of the very meaning of life itself. Israel is bound to God as the one who brought her to birth, as one who spoke to Abraham and entered into a communal plan with him to bring blessing to all the earth. Israel must be faithful to God's Torah because Torah offers the only hope for life to any human being—the only hope for a rich, full, satisfying life, one with meaning and value that will endure for all time. If Israel fails God by not keeping Torah, then Israel thereby fails herself, her forebears, her descendants, and *also all other human beings* whose health and blessing are bound up with those of Israel.

Such a depth-dimension of bondage to God and under God is involved in the notion of Israel's election. She is chosen by God as firstborn son, as one who is a *segullah,* a special treasure to God (Exod. 19:5). God loves and cares for her. God delivers her from bondage and expects gratitude, just as he expects his own love to be reciprocated. But behind and beneath all these is the work of God in the world, the plan to bring wholeness and health to all peoples and to all persons through a people whose lives are to be paradigmatic and evidentially compelling for the nations.

Normal fidelity to Torah is therefore not adequate. Normal observance of the summary prohibitions which, if violated, lead to destruction and death is not enough. No, life must be framed in such a way that no people and no person will miss the significance of Israel's bondedness to Yahweh. Viewed in such a light, the Decalogue offers such a "cement" to bind God and people together. When Israel rejects any form of worship of other gods and refuses to represent Yahweh in any kind of plastic image; when she eschews the misuse of the divine power that comes her way by virtue of her being a firstborn son and a special treasure (note the use of masculine and feminine terms); when she holds fast to Sabbath rest and shares life with aged parents; when she refuses the most evident and most powerful evidences of destructiveness to human life such as murder, adultery, thievery, false testimony, and covetousness; then she is pointing to this bond that connects her to Yahweh—one without rivals, incapable of portrayal save in his "image" (the human self), in a position to demand that his partner in the world reflect the kinds of qualities of life appropriate to the other partner and the partner's own objectives in the world.

In short, Israel is bound to Yahweh by actions of Yahweh taken long ago, actions that are themselves a part of the way of God with the world, with all creatures, especially with human beings, and most particularly with Israel, the firstborn son. Those actions of God set in motion actions within Israel that are analogous. Keeping Torah is thus no longer a matter of doing the will of one's God out of fear or gratitude or even love. It is a matter of taking one's place in a partnership of God and people, the aim of which is righteousness, peace, wholeness on earth. Therefore the whole of the creation has a stake in whether or not Israel keeps the commandments. All humankind, and certainly the Christian community (see below), should do everything possible to help Israel to be faithful to Torah. But *all* should learn the lesson of bondage to Torah. For every people and every person, to belong to God is to be in bondage to him and to his purpose. All must keep Torah, even though Israel and the church must do so in special ways and must help others to see *their* need to do so.

FREEDOM UNDER GOD

This bondage remains, but embedded within it is the deepest, most powerful gift of human freedom that the world had ever known to that time. The slaves came to freedom while remaining bound, bound now to Yahweh with cords of steel. Their life in the world is circumscribed in ways that they had not known before. The curse ritual and the specific laws of Exodus 21–23, plus later laws, surround and hem in their lives. The Decalogue gives summary expression to this new bondage. The prophets underscore it and never tire of preaching the dire consequences of failure to live as a people bound to God.

And yet Israel has now entered upon freedom, is a son and no longer a slave, a special treasure (*segullah*) and no longer booty of warfare (*shalal*), mere property, life to be used up by others to fulfill their ambitions and desires. Israel has come to freedom, freedom under God.

Keeping the commandments is such freedom. That is what we have to try to understand. For example, when Moses and those who follow him commit their lives to the observance of rest on the seventh day, they do so bound to God but also enjoying the most refreshing and liberating sense of freedom. They observe the Sabbath—to stick to this example for a while—because they are obligated to do so. This obligation is rigorous, unyielding. They cannot be who they are or live as they are appointed to live and not observe the Sabbath Day's rest. Not to rest on the seventh day is not to be what one has been made to be. It is to go against one's "nature," a nature revealed in the sacred tradition, confirmed through the centuries, and reconfirmed in our own lives.

Yet Sabbath rest is God's free gift, freely received. Who can reconcile this with the inescapable recognition of bondage to the Sabbath? Perhaps only one who has begun to observe the Sabbath, or its equivalent, in one's own tradition.

Religious devotion is a free act in at least two senses. It is my own, or our own, free commitment to do that which we are obligated by God, the all-powerful and unequal partner, to do. We decide to do what religious faith says we are required to do. That decision may therefore be coerced by the imposition of obligation under God, but when it is made by an individual, that person recognizes the act as one freely taken. When in high-pressure evangelistic meetings all the techniques of mass hypnosis, and all the slogans of a fear-ridden fundamentalistic religion, are skillfully employed, and all the pressure of a guilt-laden life is built up to force a "decision" for Christ, it must still be said that those who "decide for Christ" understand themselves freely to have chosen the decision they took. Is all that sense of freedom a delusion, an act of self-deception? Not all of it, although much of the process may be called manipulative and a dangerous use of human guilt and religious susceptibility and credulity.

Involved in even such a poor example of the witness of faith in Jesus Christ as that mentioned is a decision taken out of a desire freely to find one's life, one's very selfhood, in God. And more mature and studied decisions for Jesus Christ are all the more free acts of placing one's life in thralldom to God. So it was also for ancient Israel.

We have nothing in ancient Near Eastern religions equivalent to the response of the people to Joshua's summons to them to choose whom they would serve (Josh. 24:15). Here in a simple passage, probably reedited by the later (late seventh century) Deuteronomistic historian, is the kind of connection between bondage and freedom that the most sensitive in Israel came to understand. According to the narrative, the people had several choices. They might choose to worship God in the manner of their Mesopotamian forebears; or they might worship God in the manner of the Canaanites, among whom they were settled; or they might (and of course they should) choose to worship Yahweh, the God who had led them to this place and on whom their very lives depended. This passage has been reordered to express the rhetoric of the ceremony of renewal of the covenant. It is, however, a splendid instance of how freedom and bondage belong together. It has many equivalent instances in the New Testament literature, and it remains a classic picture of how freedom and bondage fit together religiously.

Those to whom Joshua spoke insisted that they chose to serve Yahweh. Despite warnings from Joshua that such a free act carried the most fateful consequences with it, should the people not stick to their decision, the people pressed their confession: "We *will* serve the Lord, for he is our God." Freely the people enter into bondage to Yahweh, taking upon themselves the yoke of Torah. They need not have done so, though it would have been sad indeed had they not done so. For Yahweh was the true God, and bondage to the true author and ground of all life and being is right, good, wholesome, and liberating.

The New Testament equivalents to this scene are numerous, but one that stands out is Jesus' summons: "Come to me, all who labor and are heavy laden, and I will give you rest. Take my yoke upon you, and learn from me; for I am gentle and lowly in heart, and you will find rest for your souls. For my yoke is easy, and my burden is light" (Matt. 11:28–30). The invitation can be rejected, but it should not be rejected. Once it is accepted, however, the yoke of Torah comes with it. One binds oneself in an act freely taken, and the bonds hold. But it is also right to say that God binds people to him in an act of his own, which human beings freely assent to. We give ourselves freely to God and in doing so are taken possession of by him. Or, we place ourselves in thralldom to God and in doing so come to know his gift of life and freedom!

The apostle Paul treats and illuminates this dialectic of bond-age and freedom in several of his letters. His special emphasis on enslavement to Torah and to the whole conception of works of the law should not mislead us into believing that Torah as such is the reality under attack. Paul knows a freedom in Jesus Christ that is overwhelming in its newness and in its contrast with his former life within Jewish traditional understandings of his day We can expect him to exaggerate and distort that tradition out of which he has come. He himself apparently recognizes the danger when he summons his readers not to suppose that Torah is evil or enslaving as such.[7]

Actually, Jesus and Paul show us the joy and freedom that come from being bound to God in such a way that nothing can break those bonds. Service, or *'abōdāh,* to God is our free act and, as Augustine said, it is "perfect freedom." In the com-mitment of faith to God—to God's Torah or to the Christian gospel—there is such an act of liberation, peace, joy, and ful-fillment because finally we know that we have entered the house of freedom, have become not temporary residents of a foreign land but citizens, members of God's household. The obligations of membership in the Kingdom, or the household, are a part of our very life in that kingdom, that house, and not something added to that membership. It is this kind of relationship to God that Paul calls "a new creation" (2 Cor. 5:17), a new being in which the love of Christ controls all that we are and do—our love for Christ and Christ's love for us (2 Cor. 5:14). Such a relation cannot be effectively challenged or broken by any force in the whole of creation, for it is not simply an attitude toward life, the world, ourselves, fellow human beings, or God; it is a transfiguration in the depths of our being that occurs whenever the structure of grace that includes Torah has become clear to us. When that happens, then persons formerly enslaved by the pharaohs of earth—whoever or whatever they may be—become freed and enter into a freedom that is the most inescapable bondage of all.

> Make me a captive, Lord,
> And then I shall be free;
> Force me to render up my sword,
> And I shall conqueror be.
> I sink in life's alarms
> When by myself I stand;
> Imprison me within thine arms,
> And strong shall be my hand.

It is this sense of freedom under God that the author of Psalm 119 knew. His delight in God's Torah was an almost mystical thing. He had found the way that led to life and blessing. He knew how to cope with the ambiguities and trials of life. He was bound to God by chains that would hold, and therein was he free.

We all know this sense of liberation that comes not from having broken away from old constraints and been freed from their hold (or not that alone) but from having broken *through* the barrier that separates us from true life, the light and joy and peace of God's presence, thereby leaving the bondage of enslavement or a cramped and hemmed-in life for a life in freedom that at the same time no longer allows for the damage that persons do to others or to themselves. To be sure, such damage remains possible, but action of that sort is a "kicking against the goads," an attack upon the very structure of life that means joy and peace and blessedness.

Such a sense of freedom under God depends upon the individual's participation in the life and faith of the community. It is not by any means an individual thing alone or in the first place. Just as Israel knew herself to be bound to Yahweh in covenant, so also she knew a life in association with Yahweh that was corporate. We sense the corporate joy in Yahweh in the hymns of ancient Israel, hymns in praise of God the creator such as Psalms 8, 19, and 104. The same corporate joy in God's active presence is found in such reflective psalms as Psalms 73 and 139. But the fact that Israel's prophets laid upon the people such a weight of moral demand meant that the literature of Israel outside the Psalter tends to obscure the corporate joy in relation to the gift of Torah. There was never the kind of corporate response to God's demands that satisfied the prophets; nothing would suffice but righteousness, like that which God himself would bring at the time of consummation.

In the New Testament it is the conviction that the consummation that enabled that community to take the greater corporate delight in the active presence of God had dawned. Such joy in the consummation, however, was kept alive and credible corporately. The study of the Scriptures (for the early church, the Hebrew Scriptures, of course), the identification in the Scripture of pointers to the consummation found in the one God raised from death, the life of service to one another and to the larger community, and, above all, the meals taken together that become a participation in the life of the Risen One—all these are corporate acts that enable the community to discern both the truth of the gospel and its liberating power. Bound to the one whom God has raised from death, the people also are liberated as a community from the power of sin and death by this resurrected one.

THE TEN COMMANDMENTS: CHARTER OF HUMAN FREEDOM

We now are in a position to summarize the import of the Decalogue for our own day and for any time. The Decalogue is the negative counterpart of the commandment to love God and the neighbor, and both the negative and positive forms of the commandment are essential for human beings. Taken together, they sum up for Judaism and for Christianity what it means to belong to the family, the household, of God. The neglect of the negative form of the commandments is serious indeed and can be or can become catastrophic. Without such crisp prohibitions that point unmistakably to the path that leads to death, who can hold fast to the freedom under God that these bonds entail?

None of us has sufficient moral energy to make decisions on all matters of moral activity one by one, as the occasions arise. A well-ingrained habit must govern most actions so that we do not violate the prohibitions of our relations with God or with fellow human beings because "such things are simply not done." But the habit of obedience must also be supplemented by the clear and crisp statement of what constitutes disobedience, what kinds of action, seen in an exemplary list, will surely mean ruin for us and for others. Given such a structure to ward off disobedience, one *is* free for the love of God and of neighbor in fresh ways.

For example, when a person is committed not to have sexual relations with anyone other than the spouse, such a commitment engenders trust, a freedom from anxiety, a readiness to deal with other persons who otherwise might be objects of sexual partnership in freer, more humane, less exploitative ways. A commandment such as "Thou shalt not commit adultery" is not an enslavement but a liberation, not a threat to freedom but a means to freedom, not a thwarting of life's flowering but an incentive to the flowering of human relations, including sexual relations.

Keeping the commandments thus becomes both a commitment and a habit, but such an attitude to the "law" is by no means a coercive or enslaving reality, diminishing or destroying freedom. As we have noted above, the negative form of the Decalogue is itself positive, for it leaves open, and indeed demands, the production of the positive guidelines and cases at law that make up the law collections of ancient Israel. But the summing up of the "law of love" in the Old and New Testaments in positive terms is a good counterpart to this list of ten originally negative statements. The positive law of the love of God and neighbor, like the Decalogue, very briefly and succinctly identifies the way that leads to life and peace and wholeness.

It would be a serious loss to have the positive requirements without the negative ones. The continuing witness of the Jewish people and of Jewish religious tradition is of great importance, for the Torah has the function of the Ten Commandments when the practice of dietary laws, Sabbath observance, and Jewish fidelity to Torah is not corrupted into a system of mere observances or mere regulations. If the rest of Torah observance is consciously traced back to Torah in the sense of the Decalogue, then there is little danger of a lapse into the enslavement to the law that the apostle Paul warns against—little danger for Christians or for Jews. The Decalogue has within it the heart of Torah. Positive and explicit prescriptions for life need always to be related back to and tested by the negative Ten Commandments and by the positive summary of love of God and neighbor. Such a testing of practice against this negative list is particularly important for Christian faith, because the Christian community suffers in a special way from the hidden legalisms that rush in when the community fails to see how freedom under God is related in polar tension to bondage under God.

At the present time a rebirth of commitment to the Decalogue and to its original intention and direction is desperately needed. So many of our fellow citizens and fellow Christians live lives that have no norm or direction or taste because there are no prohibitions built into our personal and social lives. With an urgency almost beyond overstatement, we need this renewal of a sense of bondage to God that will not yield to challenge. God will have his people practice faithfulness in their personal and social life. To bear false witness, to steal, to exploit the bodies of fellow men or women for our personal enjoyment, to take or to damage the life of fellow men and women, or of children, is to flaunt God's own unshakable requirements.

And though we do so, we need to know that we cannot do so. It is not a matter of building up guilt in people for their failures to keep the Law. No, the central need is for people to know two fundamental things.

The first thing people need to know is that they can have no real life, no real freedom, no real joy in life save as they lay aside the kinds of action that destroy the very things they are seeking. The Ten Commandments ward off conduct on our part which, if engaged in, will make impossible the love of God and of neighbor.

The second is the need to know that we are being drawn forward toward the day appointed by God when people will indeed avoid these prohibitions, will love God and neighbor. We need to feel the lure, the drawing power, of biblical eschatology, a drawing power that finds expression both in the negative avoidance of the actions proscribed in the Decalogue and in the positive engagement in love of God and neighbor.

This drawing power of prophetic eschatology is one of the elements held in common by Jews and Christians. Jews see the pull into a future in which God is making his own people witness more and more to the truth and power of Torah. The consummation overtakes us as we practice Torah. We are drawn by the love of God to do so, and the consummation emerges along the way and at the End—to surprise and delight us as faithfulness to Torah brings us in to the Kingdom.

The Christian has a deep sense of how in Jesus Christ that consummation has already drawn near, how the drawing power of the future has already pulled us headlong into consummation, how Torah has found its fulfillment in an internal life with God opened up in the life, teaching, suffering, death, and resurrection of Jesus the Christ. We are still drawn toward that future, but now as those who have already tasted the glories of consummation in new and fresh ways. For the Christian community, the love of God and neighbor is not only the positive demand of which the Decalogue is a negative statement; it is also a gift to us already present in our personal and social life.

But the differences are often exaggerated and too greatly drawn. Jewish eschatology too is "realized," as persons and groups place their unswerving trust in God and commit their lives to the Day that is on the way to dawning. When one knows that God is establishing peace and righteousness on a transformed earth, one already lives in that knowledge and, to a real extent, in that world to come.

To keep the commandments, then, means to live out both negatively and positively a life in the Kingdom, the full character and lineaments of which still await the final day of the Lord. Every act of faithfulness to Torah—of Sabbath-keeping, of treating elderly parents in love, of refusing to exploit another sexually or to misuse the life or goods of another—is a sign of life in the

Kingdom that already is claiming us and taking possession of us. Small moral victories thus stand in God's eyes as acts of expressed belief in the truth of God's lordship over the whole of creation.

But such a life in the Kingdom can hardly be proposed as a real possibility for individual Christian believers in isolation from a powerful community of faith. Nor can we expect the import and impact of the Decalogue to be consequential unless it is embodied in the witness of such a religious community, boldly public in its life and witness in the midst of our secular societies of the Western world. Any kind of moral commitment to the God of the covenant that does not involve the fellow believers, who together comprise God's people in the midst of the secular society, is almost sure to end in failure and disillusionment or in fanaticism and unreality. The Decalogue must contribute to the refashioning of a *communal* life under God in the world or it cannot be of assistance to us at all.

How might it do so? In my judgment, the value attributed to the provisions of the Decalogue for the individual, noted above, is greatly augmented when we think of the value such a summation of what is morally and religiously inadmissible can have for a community of faith in a secular society. The community is committed not only to the love of God and neighbor but to concrete kinds of conduct that its members pledge to one another they will not individually commit. In acts of worship, where the Decalogue provisions are presented as God's claim upon the community and where the community gives its solemn assent in covenant, much more concrete guidance is provided the community for its life in the world than one has through the glorious but too general commandment to love God and neighbor.[8]

It is this particular religious community that, in the presence of God and of fellow believers, commits itself not to fall prey to the misuse of the power God has entrusted to it, not to dishonor God's demand for rest as well as labor, not to shirk responsibility for the aged or the immature, not to commit acts of violence against the life of others or sexually to violate them, not to claim for one's own the goods God has entrusted to others, and not to be torn apart with a hankering for the life or goods of others. The community's members help one another, but the community as a whole opens up for its members this mode of life in the world as the mode God will have, a mode of life that demonstrably brings joy and gladness and a sense of purpose and meaning to those who affirm this way as the way appointed for us by God himself.

At the same time, such a corporate commitment to the Decalogue has to find response in the larger community and in its own customs and structures, if the Decalogue is to serve in the way it was intended to serve. How can such a consensus be developed in the pluralistic, secular, Western world? Here we can build upon the influence that the Decalogue and Jewish and Christian understandings of Scripture already have within the society of most Western lands. We should not underestimate the present impact within our lands of the Decalogue and of the religious understandings that produced it in ancient Israel. Already the secular members of the community are likely to give assent to the import of this set of prohibitions, when they are presented soundly and sensibly. Already they are likely to recognize that it was a remarkable moral achievement that produced the Decalogue and the prophetic heritage of ancient Israel. Our task is to build upon this disposition to understand the value of the Decalogue and what it offers to the contemporary world. The task is really twofold.

The first task is to help ourselves and our contemporary secular society recover confidence in the positive value of summary lists of human conduct that a given community (religious and secular members working together) is ready as a community to commit itself not to or no longer to practice. The way is open for such an understanding. It would be analogous to the Bill of Rights in the United States Constitution. That list of amendments has very much the form and the force of Israel's Decalogue. Certain kinds of human conduct are ruled out; they are not permitted. The community itself is committed to see to it that such conduct does not emerge. Its emergence is by that very fact a sign that the social contract, the Constitution itself, has been breached. Laws will still have to be developed to specify concretely just what the prohibitions entail, but the prohibitions themselves are one of the glorious features of the American experiment in government.

The second and by far the more difficult task is to work together, for the time necessary, to produce within the Christian community our current version of the Decalogue and to begin to benefit as a community within the secular community from its demands and guidance. We need the equivalent of these ten prohibitions, or some comparable number, for our public and private life today, both in the community of faith and in the larger society. We need just such a clean, pungent, lucid list of the kinds of corporate and individual misdeeds that bring ruin upon our society and upon its individuals. We need to frame these misdeeds in a way that will make them memorable for the children, understandable for all, and enforceable for the religious community with the very demand of the holy God himself.

This means that we are not likely to find it necessary to depart greatly from the contents of our present Decalogue, for the prohibitions in the Decalogue are earthy, rooted in the needs of human beings in society, and tied to the Jewish and Christian understandings of life in community under God. Let us attempt to list such a set of commands—they need not number ten—that has similarities and points of comparison with the ancient Decalogue.

1. Do not have more than a single ultimate allegiance.
2. Do not give ultimate loyalty to any earthly reality.
3. Do not use the power of religion to harm others.
4. Do not treat with contempt the times set aside for rest.
5. Do not treat with contempt members of the family.
6. Do not do violence against fellow human beings.
7. Do not violate the commitment of sexual love.
8. Do not claim the life or goods of others.
9. Do not damage others through misuse of human speech.
10. Do not lust after the life or goods of others.

Such a list can be supplemented by the international compacts concerning human rights that have been developed in recent years. The Universal Declaration of Human Rights, adopted by the United Nations in 1948, with its supplemental compacts and accords, offers a marvelous set of guidelines for the fulfilling of our commitment to fellow human beings in community.[9] So also do the many summary statements concerning human rights and responsibilities that have been developed by the Christian churches, some of them in direct dependence upon the Decalogue. The time is indeed right for the Christian community to reaffirm its commitment to such summary lists and to their restatement, study, and regular re-presentation within the churches.[10]

The Christian community will also know to keep vividly before itself and its members the context of love and grace within which all commandments belong and flourish. It is the incredible love and mercy of God for individual sinners, for sinful families and communities, for the church marred by sin, for the human race weighted down by the burden of sin, that enables us to understand the content and purpose of prohibitions and enables us as individuals and communally also to draw life and strength from them. But within this framework of the priority of love and grace, what can be more transfiguring for the moral existence of individuals and communities than the gift of God pointing the way for us, the way that leads to life and wholeness, the way that is nothing short of *shalom,* peace and wholeness and life as God will have life be?

APPENDIX

UNIVERSAL
DECLARATION OF
HUMAN RIGHTS

PREAMBLE

Whereas recognition of the inherent dignity and of the equal and inalienable rights of all members of the human family is the foundation of freedom, justice and peace in the world,

Whereas disregard and contempt for human rights have resulted in barbarous acts which have outraged the conscience of mankind, and the advent of a world in which human beings shall enjoy freedom of speech and belief and freedom from fear and want has been proclaimed as the highest aspiration of the common people,

Whereas it is essential, if man is not to be compelled to have recourse, as a last resort, to rebellion against tyranny and oppression, that human rights should be protected by the rule of law,

Whereas it is essential to promote the development of friendly relations between nations,

Whereas the peoples of the United Nations have in the Charter reaffirmed their faith in fundamental human rights, in the dignity and worth of the human person and in the equal rights of men and women and have determined to promote social progress and better standards of life in larger freedom,

Whereas Member States have pledged themselves to achieve, in co-operation with the United Nations, the promotion of universal respect for and observance of human rights and fundamental freedoms,

[Adopted by the United Nations in 1948.[1]]

195

Whereas a common understanding of these rights and freedoms is of the greatest importance for the full realization of this pledge,

Now, therefore,

The General Assembly

Proclaims this Universal Declaration of Human Rights as a common standard of achievement for all peoples and all nations, to the end that every individual and every organ of society, keeping this Declaration constantly in mind, shall strive by teaching and education to promote respect for these rights and freedoms and by progressive measures, national and international, to secure their universal and effective recognition and observance, both among the peoples of Member States themselves and among the peoples of territories under their jurisdiction.

ARTICLE 1

All human beings are born free and equal in dignity and rights. They are endowed with reason and conscience and should act towards one another in a spirit of brotherhood.

ARTICLE 2

Everyone is entitled to all the rights and freedoms set forth in this Declaration, without distinction of any kind, such as race, colour, sex, language, religion, political or other opinion, national or social origin, property, birth or other status.

Furthermore, no distinction shall be made on the basis of the political, jurisdictional or international status of the country or territory to which a person belongs, whether it be independent, trust, non-self-governing or under any other limitation of sovereignty.

ARTICLE 3

Everyone has the right to life, liberty and the security of person.

ARTICLE 4

No one shall be held in slavery or servitude; slavery and the slave trade shall be prohibited in all their forms.

ARTICLE 5

No one shall be subjected to torture or to cruel, inhuman or degrading treatment or punishment.

ARTICLE 6

Everyone has the right to recognition everywhere as a *person before the law*.

ARTICLE 7

All are equal before the law and are entitled *without any discrimination to equal protection of the law*. All are entitled to equal protection against any discrimination in violation of this Declaration and against any incitement to such discrimination.

ARTICLE 8

Everyone has the right to an effective remedy by the competent national tribunals for acts violating the fundamental rights granted him by the constitution or by law.

ARTICLE 9

No one shall be subjected to arbitrary arrest, detention or exile.

ARTICLE 10

Everyone is entitled in full equality to a fair and public hearing by an independent and impartial tribunal, in the determination of his rights and obligations and of any criminal charge against him.

ARTICLE 11

1. Everyone charged with a penal offense has the right to be presumed innocent until proved guilty according to law in a public trial at which he has had all the guarantees necessary for his defence.

2. No one shall be held guilty of any penal offence on account of any act or omission which did not constitute a penal offence, under national or international law, at the time when it was committed. Nor shall a heavier penalty be imposed than the one that was applicable at the time the penal offence was committed.

ARTICLE 12

No one shall be subjected to arbitrary interference with his privacy, family, home or correspondence, nor to attacks upon his honour and reputation. Everyone has the right to the protection of the law against such interference or attacks.

ARTICLE 13

1. Everyone has the right to freedom of movement and residence within the borders of each State.

2. Everyone has the right to leave any country, including his own, and to return to his country.

ARTICLE 14

1. Everyone has the right to seek and to enjoy in other countries asylum from persecution.

2. This right may not be invoked in the case of prosecutions genuinely arising from nonpolitical crimes or from acts contrary to the purposes and principles of the United Nations.

ARTICLE 15

1. *Everyone has the right to a nationality.*

2. No one shall be arbitrarily deprived of his nationality nor denied the right to change his nationality.

ARTICLE 16

1. Men and women of full age, without any limitation due to race, nationality or religion, have the *right to marry and to found a family.* They are entitled to equal rights as to marriage, during marriage and at its dissolution.

2. Marriage shall be entered into only with the free and full consent of the intending spouses.

3. The family is the natural and fundamental group unit of society and is entitled to protection by society and the State.

ARTICLE 17

1. Everyone has the right to own property alone as well as in association with others.

2. *No one shall be arbitrarily deprived of his property.*

ARTICLE 18

Everyone has the right to freedom of thought, conscience and religion; this right includes freedom to change his religion or belief, and freedom, either alone or in community with others and in public or private, to manifest his religion or belief in teaching, practice, worship and observance.

ARTICLE 19

Everyone has the right to freedom of opinion and expression; this right includes freedom to hold opinions without interference and to seek, receive and impart information and ideas through any media and regardless of frontiers.

ARTICLE 20

1. Everyone has the right to freedom of peaceful assembly and association.

2. No one may be compelled to belong to an association.

ARTICLE 21

1. Everyone has the right to take part in the government of his country, directly or through freely chosen representatives.

2. Everyone has the right of equal access to public service in his country.

3. The will of the people shall be the basis of the authority of government; this will shall be expressed in periodic and genuine elections which shall be by universal and equal suffrage and shall be held by secret vote or by equivalent free voting procedures.

ARTICLE 22

Everyone, as a member of society, has the right to social security and is entitled to realization, through national effort and international co-operation and in accordance with the organization and resources of each state, of the economic, social and cultural rights indispensable for his dignity and the free development of his personality.

ARTICLE 23

1. Everyone has the right to work, to free choice of employ-

ment, to just and favourable conditions of work and to protection against unemployment.

2. Everyone, without any discrimination, has the right to equal pay for equal work.

3. Everyone who works has the right to just and favourable remuneration ensuring for himself and his family an existence worthy of human dignity, and supplemented, if necessary, by other means of social protection.

4. Everyone has the right to form and to join trade unions for the protection of his interests.

ARTICLE 24

Everyone has the right to rest and leisure, including reasonable limitation of working hours and periodic holidays with pay.

ARTICLE 25

1. Everyone has the right to a standard of living adequate for the health and well-being of himself and of his family, including food, clothing, housing and medical care and necessary social services, and the right to security in the event of unemployment, sickness, disability, widowhood, old age or other lack of livelihood in circumstances beyond his control.

2. Motherhood and childhood are entitled to special care and assistance. All children, whether born in or out of wedlock, shall enjoy the same social protection.

ARTICLE 26

1. *Everyone has the right to education.* Education shall be free, at least in the elementary and fundamental stages. *Elementary education shall be compulsory.* Technical and professional education shall be made generally available and higher education shall be equally accessible to all on the basis of merit.

2. *Education shall be directed to the full development of the human personality* and to the strengthening of respect for human rights and fundamental freedoms. It shall promote understanding, tolerance and friendship among all nations, racial or religious groups, and shall further the activities of the United Nations for the maintenance of peace.

3. Parents have a prior right to choose the kind of education that shall be given to their children.

ARTICLE 27

1. Everyone has the right freely to participate in the cultural life of the community, to enjoy the arts and to share in scientific advancement and its benefits.

2. Everyone has the right to the protection of the moral and material interests resulting from any scientific, literary or artistic production of which he is the author.

ARTICLE 28

Everyone is entitled to a social and international order in which the rights and freedoms set forth in this Declaration can be fully realized.

ARTICLE 29

1. Everyone has duties to the community in which alone the free and full development of his personality is possible.

2. In the exercise of his rights and freedoms, everyone shall be subject only to such limitations as are determined by law solely for the purpose of securing due recognition and respect for the rights and freedoms of others and of meeting the just requirements of morality, public order and the general welfare in a democratic society.

3. These rights and freedoms may in no case be exercised contrary to the purposes and principles of the United Nations.

ARTICLE 30

Nothing in this Declaration may be interpreted as implying for any State, group or person any right to engage in any activity or to perform any act aimed at the destruction of any of the rights and freedoms set forth herein.

Notes

PREFACE

1. See especially my "Ten Commandments," *IDB* 4 (1962): 569–73; and "Law, in the OT," *IDB* 3 (1962): 77–89.

2. Gerhard Ebeling, *Die zehn Gebote in Predigten ausgelegt* (Tübingen: Mohr, 1973).

3. Helen Schüngel-Straumann, *Der Dekalog–Gebot Gottes?* Stuttgarter Bibelstudien 67, ed. H. Haag, R. Kilian, and W. Pesch (Stuttgart: KBW Verlag, 1973).

4. See the excellent article by Moshe Greenberg, "Decalogue," in *Encyclopaedia Judaica* 5 (Jerusalem: Keter Publishing House, 1971), cols. 1435–46.

CHAPTER 1: THE TEN COMMANDMENTS TODAY

1. Gerhard Ebeling, *Die zehn Gebote in Predigten ausgelegt* (Tübingen: Mohr, 1973).

2. See Calvin's marvelous exposition on the Ten Commandments in the *Institutes,* bk. 2, chap. 8. I am using the edition translated by John Allen, *Institutes of the Christian Religion* (Philadelphia: Board of Christian Education, 1936), 1:396–457.

3. See my "The Biblical Concept of the Free Man," *Review and Expositor* 57 (1960): 263–80. See also my study of prophetic eschatology in *Lifeboat Ethics: The Moral Dilemmas of World Hunger,* ed. George R. Lucas, Jr., and Thomas W. Ogletree (New York: Harper & Row, 1976), pp. 84–99.

4. See George E. Mendenhall's highly influential study, *Law and Covenant in Israel and the Ancient Near East* (Pittsburgh:

The Biblical Colloquium, 1955), first published in *BA* 17 (1954): 26–45, 50–75.

5. Anthony Phillips, *Ancient Israel's Criminal Law: A New Approach to the Decalogue* (Oxford: Blackwell, 1970).

CHAPTER 2: THE ORIGIN, STRUCTURE, AND
SETTING OF THE TEN COMMANDMENTS

1. Eduard Nielsen, *The Ten Commandments in New Perspective*, SBT 2,7 (Chicago: Allenson, 1968).

2. See Johann Jakob Stamm with Maurice Edward Andrew, *The Ten Commandments in Recent Research*, SBT 2,2 (Chicago: Allenson, 1967).

3. Erhard Gerstenberger, *Wesen und Herkunft des "Apodiktischen Rechts,"* WMANT 20, ed. G. Bornkamm and G. von Rad (Neukirchen/Vluyn: Neukirchener Verlag, 1965).

4. See especially Albrecht Alt, "The Origins of Israelite Law," in *Essays on Old Testament History and Religion* (Garden City, N.Y.: Doubleday, 1966), pp. 79–132.

5. George E. Mendenhall, *Law and Covenant in Israel and the Ancient Near East* (Pittsburgh: The Biblical Colloquium, 1955).

6. Klaus Baltzer, *The Covenant Formulary in Old Testament, Jewish, and Early Christian Writings,* trans. David E. Green (Philadelphia: Fortress Press, 1971), translated from the 2d edition of *Das Bundesformular,* WMANT 4 (Neukirchen/Vluyn: Neukirchener Verlag, 1964).

7. Anthony Phillips, *Ancient Israel's Criminal Law: A New Approach to the Decalogue* (Oxford: Blackwell, 1970).

8. Brevard S. Childs, *The Book of Exodus: A Critical, Theological Commentary* (Philadelphia: Westminster Press, 1974).

9. J. Philip Hyatt, *Exodus,* New Century Bible (London: Oliphants, 1971).

10. John Van Seters, *Abraham in History and Tradition* (New Haven: Yale University Press, 1975).

11. See note 4, above.

12. See Gerstenberger, *Wesen und Herkunft des "Apodiktischen Rechts,"* pp. 130–38.

13. English translations of the most important of these legal materials are found in *ANET*, pp. 159–223.

14. See *ANET*, pp. 212–17.

15. Dennis J. McCarthy, *Treaty and Covenant*, Analecta Biblica 21 (Rome: Pontifical Biblical Institute, 1963).

16. Gerstenberger, *Wesen und Herkunft des "Apodiktischen Rechts,"* pp. 135–37.

17. See especially Gerhard Liedke, *Gestalt und Bezeichnung alttestamentlicher Rechtssätze*, WMANT 39 (Neukirchen/Vluyn: Neukirchener Verlag, 1971).

18. Ibid., pp. 154–200.

19. See especially Willy Schottroff, *Der altisraelitische Fluchspruch*, WMANT 30 (Neukirchen/Vluyn: Neukirchener Verlag, 1969); Stanley Gevirtz, *Patterns in the Early Poetry of Israel*, Studies in Ancient Oriental Civilization 32 (Chicago: University of Chicago Press, 1963); idem, "West Semitic Curses and the Problem of the Origins of Hebrew Law," *VT* 11 (1961): 137–58; W. J. Harrelson, "Blessings and Cursings," *IDB* 1: 446–48. Schottroff has a full and excellent bibliography.

20. Schottroff, *Der altisraelitische Fluchspruch*, pp. 231–33, concludes his detailed investigation with the observation that the curse, like the blessing, is by no means tied to the cult. Distinctive Israelite formulations of the curse are a means of excluding offenders from the clan or tribe and thereby maintaining its health. When the Israelites are established in Canaan and subject to Canaanite influences, the magical powers of the curse and the cultic connections become more pronounced.

21. Ibid., pp. 211–17.

22. Gevirtz, "West Semitic Curses and the Problem of the Origins of Hebrew Law," pp. 137–58. Gevirtz also shows the close connection between the casuistic and the apodictic styles of law in this study.

23. See also Dennis J. McCarthy, *Old Testament Covenant: A Survey of Current Opinions* (Richmond: John Knox Press, 1972).

24. See Walter Harrelson, *The City of Shechem: Its History and Importance* (Ann Arbor, Mich.: University Microfilms,

1953), pp. 315–404, for an effort to reconstruct this ritual act and to show its significance.

25. See Martin Noth's treatment of this Hebrew expression in *Das System der Zwölf Stämme Israels,* BWAT 4,1 (Stuttgart: W. Kohlhammer, 1930).

26. See Stanley Gevirtz, "Curse," *IDB* 1: 749–50. See also Harrelson, "Blessings and Cursings." Schottroff, *Der altisraelitische Fluchspruch,* pp. 231–33, believes that the form *'arur* was originally an Israelite form of the curse.

27. Harrelson, *The City of Shechem,* pp. 315–404.

28. The most recent comprehensive study is that by Jörn Halbe, *Das Privilegrecht Jahwes, Ex 34,10–26,* Gestalt und Wesen, Herkunft und Wirken in vordeuteronomischer Zeit, FRLANT 114 (Göttingen: Vandenhoeck und Ruprecht, 1975).

29. Nielsen, *The Ten Commandments in New Perspective,* p. 30.

30. Ibid., pp. 17–19.

31. See Walther Zimmerli, *Ezechiel,* Biblischer Kommentar, Altes Testament XIII, 1 (Neukirchen/Vluyn: Neukirchener Verlag; 1969), pp. 391–416; Nielsen, *The Ten Commandments in New Perspective,* pp. 25–26.

32. Sigmund Mowinckel, *Psalmenstudien V: Segen und Fluch in Israels Kult und Psalmdichtung* (Kristiania: Jacob Dybwad, 1924).

33. See Gerhard von Rad on Psalms 15 and 24 in his essay " 'Gerechtigkeit' und 'Leben' in der Kultsprache der Psalmen," *Gesammelte Studien zum Alten Testament,* TB 8 (Munich: Kaiser, 1958), pp. 225–47.

34. See Kurt Galling on the term *Beichtspiegel* (confessional mirror) in *ZAW* 47 (1929): 125.

35. Nielsen, *The Ten Commandments in New Perspective,* pp. 78–86. The Hebrew text behind this translation of Nielsen is as follows:

1. לא תשתחוה לאל אחר
2. לא תעשה לך פסל
3. לא תשא את־שם יהוה לשוא
4. לא תעשה מלאכה ביום השבת

5. לֹא תְקַלֶּה אֶת־אָבִיךָ וְאֶת־אִמֶּךָ
6. לֹא תִנְאַף אֶת־אֵשֶׁת רֵעֶךָ
7. לֹא תִשְׁפֹּךְ אֶת־דַּם רֵעֶךָ
8. לֹא תִגְנֹב אִישׁ מֵרֵעֶךָ
9. לֹא תַעֲנֶה בְרֵעֶךָ עֵד שָׁקֶר
10. לֹא תַחְמֹד בֵּית רֵעֶךָ

36. Well set forth by Albrecht Alt, "Das Verbot des Diebstahls im Dekalog," in *Kleine Schriften zur Geschichte des Volkes Israel* (Munich: Beck, 1953), 1:333–40.

37. The Hebrew text is as follows:

1. לֹא יִהְיֶה לְךָ אֱלֹהִים אֲחֵרִים
2. לֹא תַעֲשֶׂה לְךָ פֶסֶל
3. לֹא תִשָּׂא אֶת־שֵׁם יְהוָה לַשָּׁוְא
4. לֹא תְקַלֶּה אֶת־יוֹם הַשַּׁבָּת
5. לֹא תְקַלֵּל אֶת־אָבִיךָ וְאֶת־אִמֶּךָ
6. לֹא תִרְצַח אֶת־רֵעֶךָ
7. לֹא תִנְאַף אֶת־אֵשֶׁת רֵעֶךָ
8.* לֹא תִגְנֹב אֶת־כֹּל אֲשֶׁר לְרֵעֶךָ
9. לֹא תַעֲנֶה בְרֵעֶךָ עֵד שָׁקֶר
10. לֹא תַחְמֹד בֵּית רֵעֶךָ

38. J. Philip Hyatt, *Exodus,*, pp. 195–99.

39. See my "Worship in Ancient Israel," *Biblical Research* 3 (1958): 1–14. See also my *From Fertility Cult to Worship* (Garden City, N.Y.: Doubleday, 1969), pp. 80–95 (reprinted by Scholars Press, Missoula, Mont., pp. 101–20).

40. See Bo Reicke, *Die zehn Worte in Geschichte und Gegenwart. Zählung und Bedeutung in den verschiedenen Konfessionen,* Beiträge zur Geschichte der biblischen Exegese, 13 (Tübingen: Mohr, 1973). For the numbering of the commandments in the Orthodox church, see Athenagoras Kokkinakis (Archbishop of Thyateira and Great Britain), *The Thyateira Confession: The Faith and Prayer of the People of God, in English and Greek* (Leighton Buzzard, Beds.: Faith Press, 1975), pp. 120–30.

*We could, and perhaps should, eliminate the כֹּל and simply read:
לֹא תִגְנֹב אֶת־אֲשֶׁר לְרֵעֶךָ

CHAPTER 3: GOD'S EXCLUSIVE CLAIMS

1. See the denunciations of the foreign nations by Amos in 1:3—2:3. These do not necessarily mean that Amos believed Israel's covenant law to apply to all peoples. The denunciations do suggest that the prophet, apparently quite unselfconsciously, recognized that the moral demands of Israel's God in some way claimed other peoples as well as Israel.

2 See especially the article by Walther Zimmerli, "Ich bin Jahwe," first published in 1953 and reprinted in *Gottes Offenbarung: Gesammelte Aufsätze zum Alten Testament,* TB 19 (Munich: Kaiser, 1963), pp. 11–40.

3. See Dennis J. McCarthy, *Old Testament Covenant: A Survey of Current Opinions* (Richmond: John Knox Press, 1972), pp. 15–20.

4. See the highly suggestive book by Peter L. Berger, *A Rumor of Angels: Modern Society and the Rediscovery of the Supernatural* (Garden City, N.Y.: Doubleday, 1969), pp. 88–89.

5. Brevard S. Childs, *The Book of Exodus: A Critical Theological Commentary* (Philadelphia: Westminster Press, 1974), p. 403.

6. See Hans Küng, *Existiert Gott?* (Munich: R. Piper, 1978), for a detailed discussion of issues concerning belief in God in the contemporary world.

7. See my discussion in *From Fertility Cult to Worship* (Garden City, N.Y.: Doubleday, 1969), pp. 90–92.

8. See K.-H. Bernhardt, *Gott und Bild: Ein Beitrag zur Begründung und Deutung des Bilderverbots im Alten Testament* (Berlin: Evangelische Verlagsanstalt, 1956).

9. See my "The Significance of Cosmology in the Ancient Near East," in *Translating and Understanding the Old Testament,* ed. H. T. Frank and W. L. Reed (Nashville: Abingdon Press, 1970), pp. 237–52.

10. See Gerhard von Rad, *Old Testament Theology* (New York: Harper & Row, 1962), 1: 212–19.

11. *Institutes,* bk. 2, chap. 8.

12. See Walther Zimmerli, "Das Bildverbot in der Geschichte

des alten Israel (Goldenes Kalb, Eherne Schlange, Mazzeben und Lade)," in *Schalom: Studien zu Glaube und Geschichte Israels,* ed. K.-H. Bernhardt, Arbeiten zur Theologie 1,46 (Stuttgart: Calwer Verlag, 1971), pp. 86–96.

13. The use of the term *son* for Israel is paralleled by the use of bridal and other female terminology in other places, as will be evident in the discussion below.

14. Eduard Nielsen, *The Ten Commandments in New Perspective,* SBT 2,7 (Chicago: Allenson, 1968), pp. 88, 128–38.

15. The deaths in November 1978 of the Reverend James Jones and the members of his "People's Temple" in Jonestown, Guyana, come readily to mind.

16. Exodus 3:13–18; 33:12–23; 34:5–7.

CHAPTER 4: GOD'S BASIC INSTITUTIONS

1. The vast literature on the origin and meaning of the Sabbath is well summed up in Niels-Erik A. Andreasen, *The Old Testament Sabbath: A Traditio-Historical Investigation,* SBL Dissertation Series 7 (Missoula, Mont.: Scholars Press, 1972).

2. See Willy Rordorf, *Sunday: The History of the Day of Rest and Worship in the Earliest Centuries of the Christian Church* (Philadelphia: Westminster Press, 1968).

3. Hans-Joachim Kraus, *Worship in Israel: A Cultic History of the Old Testament* (Richmond: John Knox Press, 1966), pp. 78–88.

4. Eduard Nielsen, *The Ten Commandments in New Perspective,* SBT 2,7 (Chicago: Allenson, 1968), pp. 102–3.

5. Rordorf, *Sunday,* pp. 12–20, whose observations are excellent but somewhat one-sided.

6. See Walter Brueggemann, *The Land* (Philadelphia: Fortress Press, 1977), pp. 63–65, for excellent observations on the importance of the Sabbath for the social life of humankind.

7. See Hans Walter Wolff, *Anthropology of the Old Testament* (Philadelphia: Fortress Press, 1974), pp. 128–42.

8. Among many passages, see Prov. 6:6–11, 24:30–34, and 26:13–16.

9. See Gen. 34:7; Judg. 19:23, 30; 2 Sam. 13:12.

CHAPTER 5: BASIC HUMAN OBLIGATIONS

1. See Gerhard von Rad, *Der Heilige Krieg im alten Israel,* ATANT 20 (Zurich: Zwingli-Verlag, 1951).

2. See Karl Barth, *Church Dogmatics* (Edinburgh: T. & T. Clark, 1957), 2,2: 683–86; 3,4: 47–564. See also my "Karl Barth on the Decalogue," *Studies in Religion* 6 (1976–77): 229–40.

3. The cult of the dead may have flourished in ancient Israel more widely than scholars had supposed. See Marvin H. Pope, *Song of Songs,* Anchor Bible (Garden City, N.Y.: Doubleday, 1977), pp. 210–29.

4. See my "Famine in the Perspective of Biblical Judgments and Promises," in *Lifeboat Ethics: The Moral Dilemmas of World Hunger,* ed. George R. Lucas, Jr., and Thomas W. Ogletree (New York: Harper & Row, 1976), pp. 88–89.

5. See note 2, above.

6. It is often pointed out that a woman becomes an adulteress by Old Testament definition in relation to her own betrothal or marriage, while a man becomes an adulterer in relation to the marriage of another couple.

7. See my "The Significance of Cosmology in the Ancient Near East," in *Translating and Understanding the Old Testament,* ed. H. T. Frank and W. L. Reed (Nashville: Abingdon Press, 1970), passim.

8. Excellent observations on the commandment against adultery are found in Helen Schüngel-Straumann, *Der Dekalog— Gebot Gottes?* Stuttgarter Bibelstudien 67, ed. H. Haag, R. Kilian, and W. Pesch (Stuttgart: KBW Verlag, 1973), pp. 47–53, 114–18.

CHAPTER 6: BASIC SOCIAL OBLIGATIONS

1. Notably Albrecht Alt, "Das Verbot des Diebstahls im Dekalog, in *Kleine Schriften zur Geschichte des Volkes Israel* (Munich: Beck, 1953), 1:330–40.

2. See J. Philip Hyatt, New Century Bible (London: Oliphants, 1971), pp. 216–17, for an excellent discussion of the meaning of the Hebrew term *ḥamad.*

3. See note 1, above.

4. See, e.g., Prov. 6:17, 12:19, 22.

5. See *ANET,* pp. 407–10 (the tale of the "eloquent peasant"), and 412–18 (the instructions of Ptah-Hotep and of Meri-Ka-Re).

6. On the "secularity" or "worldliness" of biblical religion, and especially of the Old Testament, see Walther Zimmerli, *Die Weltlichkeit des Alten Testaments* (Göttingen: Vandenhoeck und Ruprecht, 1971); Walter Brueggemann, *In Man We Trust* (Richmond: John Knox Press, 1972).

CHAPTER 7: THE TEN COMMANDMENTS
AND THE NEW TESTAMENT

1. Very important work is being done today on the Deuteronomistic traditions. See Moshe Weinfeld, *Deuteronomy and the Deuteronomic School* (Oxford: Clarendon, 1972); Timo Veijola, *Die ewige Dynastie: David und die Entstehung seiner Dynastie nach der deuteronomistischen Darstellung* (Helsinki: Suomalainen Tiedeakatemia, 1975).

2. Martin Noth, *The Laws in the Pentateuch and Other Studies,* trans. D. R. Ap-Thomas (Philadelphia: Fortress Press, 1967), pp. 85–103. See also my "Law, in the OT," *IDB* 3 (1962): 77.

3. See the many writings of W. D. Davies on this theme, and particularly his *Paul and Rabbinic Judaism: Some Rabbinical Elements in Pauline Theology* (London: SPCK, 1970) and *Torah in the Messianic Age and/or the Age to Come,* JBL Monograph Series 7 (Philadelphia: Society of Biblical Literature, 1952).

4. See Krister Stendahl, *Paul among Jews and Gentiles and Other Essays* (Philadelphia: Fortress Press, 1976).

5. See Martin Buber, *Two Types of Faith* (London: Routledge and Kegan Paul, 1951).

6. See Rudolf Bultmann, *Theology of the New Testament* (New York: Scribner's, 1951), 1: 259–69.

7. See especially Rom. 2:12—8:39.

8. Romans 7:7–25.

9. See Hans Küng, *On Being a Christian* (Garden City, N.Y.: Doubleday, 1976), for a powerful and eloquent restatement.

CHAPTER 8: THE TEN COMMANDMENTS IN RELIGIOUS LIFE TODAY

1. My colleague Douglas A. Knight is at work on a new approach to the study of biblical ethics, with the assistance of other biblical scholars and ethicists.

2. See the classic work by H. H. Rowley, *The Biblical Doctrine of Election* (London: Lutterworth, 1950).

3. See Gerhard von Rad, *Genesis: A Commentary,* trans. John H. Marks, Old Testament Library (Philadelphia: Westminster Press, 1961), pp. 150–56.

4. See my "Famine in the Perspective of Biblical Judgments and Promises," in *Lifeboat Ethics: The Moral Dilemmas of World Hunger,* ed. George R. Lucas, Jr., and Thomas W. Ogletree (New York: Harper & Row, 1976), p. 97.

5. This picture of Zion's rise from the flames and ashes continues after A.D. 70. See 2 Esdras 9–10 and my essay in *The Divine Helmsman: Studies on God's Control of Human Events, Presented to Lou H. Silberman,* ed. James L. Crenshaw and Samuel Sandmel (New York: KTAV Publishing Company, 1980), pp. 21–40.

6. See Jürgen Moltmann, *Theology of Hope* (New York: Harper & Row, 1967); and idem, *The Experiment Hope* (Philadelphia: Fortress Press, 1975).

7. Romans 7:7–12, 11:29.

8. See my *From Fertility Cult to Worship* (Garden City, N.Y.: Doubleday, 1969), pp. 106–8.

9. See the Appendix. See also *The United Nations and Human Rights,* an excellent study by James Frederick Green (Washington: The Brookings Institution, 1956).

10. I think the focus should be the Christian community, although the relations between Judaism and Christianity and between Islam and Christianity must be kept constantly in view as this effort within the Christian community takes place. I am also quite hopeful that the confrontation can go on to include

the other great religions of humankind. Peter L. Berger has some provocative things to say on that subject in *The Heretical Imperative* (Garden City, N.Y.: Doubleday, 1979), pp. 125–89.

APPENDIX: UNIVERSAL DECLARATION OF HUMAN RIGHTS

1. Several draft covenants, plus compacts and accords produced since this 1948 Declaration, show the continuing influence of this marvelous document and also reveal how difficult it is to secure full adoption and compliance with the Declaration. See James Frederick Green, *The United Nations and Human Rights* (Washington: The Brookings Institution, 1956), Appendix A, pp. 175–78, for the above text of the Declaration. For a fresh study of the Universal Declaration and its import today, see *Understanding Human Rights: An Interdisciplinary and Interfaith Study,* ed. Alan D. Falconer (Dublin: Irish School of Ecumenics, 1980).

Indexes

SCRIPTURE REFERENCES

215

AUTHORS, EDITORS, AND TRANSLATORS

SUBJECTS